OXFORD
INDIA SHORT
INTRODUCTIONS

INDIAN CITIES

The Oxford India Short
Introductions are concise,
stimulating, and accessible guides
to different aspects of India.
Combining authoritative analysis,
new ideas, and diverse perspectives,
they discuss subjects which are
topical yet enduring, as also
emerging areas of study and debate.

A part of the *Oxford India Short Introductions* series, this book belongs to a cluster of nine titles around the theme 'Economics and Development'. I have deliberately kept these two words separate. We tend to forget that the non-economic aspects of development have an important bearing on the economic aspects. The focus of the theme is how a country like India faces and solves (or fails to solve) various questions related to its quest for sustainable development. Moreover, every book within this cluster presents the reader with a quick recapitulation of the relevant theory so that opinions can be disentangled from conclusions based on theory.

Anindya Sen, Professor of Economics, Indian Institute of Management Calcutta; General Editor for the cluster on 'Economics and Development', *OISI*

Forthcoming Titles in the Cluster

Monetary Policy
Partha Ray

Capital Flows and Exchange Rate Management
Soumyen Sikdar

Trade and Environment
Rajat Acharyya

OXFORD
INDIA SHORT
INTRODUCTIONS

INDIAN
CITIES

ANNAPURNA SHAW

OXFORD
UNIVERSITY PRESS

Oxford University Press is a department of the University of Oxford.
It furthers the University's objective of excellence in research, scholarship,
and education by publishing worldwide. Oxford is a registered trademark of
Oxford University Press in the UK and in certain other countries

Published in India
by Oxford University Press
22 Workspace, 2nd Floor, 1/22 Asaf Ali Road, New Delhi 110002, India

ISBN-13: 978-0-19-807536-3
ISBN-10: 0-19-807536-7

Typeset in 11/15.6 Bembo Std
by Excellent Laser Typesetters, Pitampura, Delhi 110 034
Printed in India by Replika Press Pvt. Ltd.

To Purnea
the small town where I grew up
and to Kolkata and Mumbai
for that sense of place and belonging
of my later years

Contents

Tables and Figures

Tables

Figures

Acknowledgements

I must begin by thanking Nitasha Devasar for suggesting that a book on Indian cities be written for the general reader. As an academic, I had not thought that such a book might be of interest to anyone outside academia. I must also thank Anindya Sen—General Editor for the cluster on 'Economics and Development' in the *Oxford India Short Introductions* series—for his constant encouragement and useful suggestions to enhance the book's readability.

Mayak Sen, former CMIE (Centre for Monitoring Indian Economy) analyst at the IIMC (Indian Institute of Management Calcutta) library, helped me immensely by extracting important data from the CMIE Capex databank and arranging it by leading cities. Anjusri Bhattacharya, a cartographer working at CSSS (Centre

Acknowledgements

for Studies in the Social Sciences), Kolkata, made the maps that have been used in this book. My thanks to both of them and to the editorial team at Oxford University Press.

I am also very grateful to my husband Debashish and son Arjun who, as always, were so encouraging and supportive. Their interest in cities, both here and abroad, was an added reason to write this book.

Introduction

As for many developing nations, the twenty-first century will be India's urban century, a period during which
its population will become overwhelmingly urban. In
1901, there were just around 26 million people living
in urban areas and they accounted for roughly 11 per
cent of India's population. The remaining 89 per cent
were living in villages scattered throughout the country. With independence in 1947 and the development
policies of the nationalist state, movement to towns
and cities accelerated and gradually the percentage of
the country's population living in urban areas began
to increase. Provisional results of the Census of 2011
indicate that it is now at around 31 per cent. This is
still fairly low when compared to most other large
developing countries because, on the whole, during

the last century, the rate of urbanization has been sluggish. The percentage of the country's population living in urban areas increased quite slowly with the majority of people still living in rural areas. But even these small percentage increases resulted in the addition of huge numbers of people and today India's urban population of 377 million is more than the total population of the United States. Moreover, the pace of urbanization is likely to quicken in the next three to four decades with the deepening impact of globalization, rising literacy, depleting natural resources, and a declining agricultural sector. These factors will strengthen the so-called 'aspirational' drivers to urbanization as towns and cities, more and more, represent new opportunities and the fulfilment of aspirations for the younger generation.

Projections of India's urban population for 2026 made by the census registrar general's office anticipate 534 million people, a near doubling of the 2001 figure. In 2011, at 377 million, there has been an addition of 90 million people during the last decade. In fact while the decadal growth for urban areas during 2001–11 was 37 per cent, it was only 12 per cent for rural areas. With lower rates of rural population growth and a declining agricultural economy, it is clear that in the twenty-first century, towns and cities are going to become the dominant living environment of India's millions. As the urban environment takes centre stage, there will be a new interest in towns and cities and what makes them work.

As has been noted in the voluminous work of the last century, the urbanization of the developing world and its giant sprawling cities is different from that of the West. For decades, cities in poor countries have been regarded as a kind of misfit representation of the real city and their modernity, a kind of inauthentic, borrowed modernity. With so many poor people, slums and squatter settlements, lack of rules regarding land use, chaotic and disorderly growth, their existence and future have always been questioned by experts and contrasted to the proper cities or the well-planned and managed cities of the West. But as the economies in which some of these cities are located began to do better and to even exceed the economic growth of the West, there has been a new interest in the cities of the South. How can so much squalor and wealth exist side by side? Why do world-class companies locate in these cities when there are no proper roads? How do these cities so easily absorb such a diverse population speaking many languages and practising many religions and yet are not able to provide proper sanitation? Why are they modern in parts only, with some city quarters unchanged for the last hundred years? These and other similar questions have necessitated a slowly changing focus and a different lens with which to examine these cities, namely, the acceptance of the notion of an alternative modernity or an 'indigenous modernity', which enables us to see and understand them as they are, products of their own complex and hybrid pasts and not just against some normative template established by the experiences of the West.

One of the aims of this book is to elucidate the Indian city through this alternative lens highlighting not only the organized and planned built environment but also the informal processes of city-building and the presence of the large informal sector in the city's economy. Keeping in mind that the Indian city is much more complex an entity than it was even two or three decades ago, formality and informality in the city are likely to reveal new intersections and spatial manifestations. Not only is the Indian city of today much larger in size, both physically and in population numbers, but it is also a product of two decades of economic liberalization and globalization. Since 1991, when the Indian economy was opened to the outside world and liberalization policies adopted by the central government, profound changes have been taking place. While some of the changes are visible on the urban landscape and can be easily observed, many others have just started or have not gone through their full course and their impacts are still unknown. Or they are subtle changes in organizations and institutions that are less visible but with impacts on everyday life. This book sheds light on some of these visible and not-so-visible changes and incorporates them in its exposition of the Indian city.

From looking at the different kinds of changes our cities are undergoing, it is also necessary to have an understanding of their depth and extent. This leads to another question of interest which is to what extent are Indian cities becoming 'generic cities', that is, adopting the built-environment format of large parts of USA with its penchant for steel and glass towers in the business districts, identical retail and restaurant franchises, and transport systems based primarily on the automobile, and to what extent do they continue to retain a type of urbanism rooted in India's cultural history.

While the former process brings along certain conveniences to the upwardly mobile middle class, global business, and global clients in the easily recognizable and the familiar, it also implies a certain loss of diversity and cultural uniqueness that enhance the experience of urban living.

One of the difficulties of writing a generalized account of cities or large urban settlements is that they are always in motion and ever-changing. This idea as highlighted by Mehrotra (2008) is embedded in the notion of the 'kinetic city' or the city of impermanence and temporary structures. In the developing country context, the latter would include slum dwellings, informal markets, and the entire urban informal sector and its multiple economies. While standard writing can cover the static city or the city of the established built environment, it is more difficult to capture the realities of the kinetic city. Yet it is also very much a part of the total urban living experience of Indian cities where it is intertwined in myriad and inexplicable ways to the established or permanent city.

Finally, for a proper understanding of the Indian city, it will be necessary to go beyond an understanding of its physical structure or its built environment and land uses, to an understanding of its residents, who they are and how they live. Without this human and social dimension, no generalized account of the Indian city would be complete or interesting.

Keeping these considerations in mind, the following is a chapter-by-chapter organization of this book. In Chapter 1, a brief history of the Indian city is presented with a discussion of pre-colonial and colonial developments and the city of the post-independence era up to 1991. It is followed by Chapter 2 which focuses on the city in the post-economic-liberalization era, the drivers of urban growth during this period and their effects on city size and structure. Chapter 3 highlights the economic activities of Indian cities focusing on both the formal economy as well as the informal economy. Chapter 4 asks why Indian cities look the way they do with their disorderly mix of land use, building heights, and architectural styles. To answer this, it is necessary to understand their cultural histories, government policies, and demographic growth. Chapter 5 expands on these aspects by looking at the social milieu of Indian cities and asking whether they are melting pots or enclaves and to what extent they enable mobility and new identities. In Chapter 6 comes the all-important question

about the quality of life in Indian cities and the condition of their basic urban services, health and education
facilities. Chapter 7 which concludes the book turns to
the overall liveability of Indian cities, their future, and
what must be done to improve their inclusiveness and
maintain their economic and cultural diversity.

Scope of the Work

It is important, at the beginning of this book, to first
clarify what is meant by the 'Indian city' and thereby
to establish the scope of the work. This is all the more
necessary given the huge size of India's urban population and the range in size of its urban places. According
to the Census of 2001, India had 286 million people
living in 5,161 urban places. The provisional results of
the Census of 2011 indicate that this has gone up to 377
million people living in over 7,000 urban places. The
largest, the Greater Mumbai Municipal Corporation
had a population of 11.9 million in 2001 while the
smallest had a population size just exceeding 2,000 as
in Khawhai (2,403) and Lengpui (2,423) in Mizoram.

According to the census, a 'city' is an urban place
with a population of 100,000 and above. This defini-

tion has both advantages and disadvantages. It gives us around 500 cities, in 2011, with a wide range in population size, and economic and social composition. Most of the Indian states, barring Sikkim and Arunachal Pradesh, have at least one such urban place. However, those cities at the top of the Indian urban system with populations exceeding 5 million are urban giants or mega cities while those at the borderline of the cut-off of 100,000 are more like small towns. The census definition, while having the advantage of being broad and geographically inclusive, has the disadvantage of clubbing together settlements that are too different from each other and not comparable in terms of the services they offer, their physical and demographic size and their structural complexity. Urban settlements at the upper end offer a range of higher order goods and services that cannot be found in a settlement of 100,000 or 200,000, for instance, a university, museums, art galleries, zoos, and specialty hospitals. Travelling from one end of a large city to the other on a daily basis is time-consuming and rents and overall costs of living are higher than in smaller urban places. Life is faster and more frenetic and there is a trade-off between more educational and job opportunities on the one hand and greater noise, pollution, and lack of green spaces, on the other.

Keeping these differences in mind, it is useful to think in terms of large, medium, and small cities. While the background chapters have been written with all urban places in mind, this book has a restricted focus for later chapters. Here the discussion and the material used are confined to the large city. Any urban settlement with a population of 1 million and above is considered a large city. About this, there is considerable unanimity in the academic literature in India. There is less agreement about what constitutes a medium-sized city and a small city but on the whole, urban places with a population of less than 1 million to 500,000 can be regarded as medium-sized cities and those between 500,000 and 100,000 as small cities. Below 100,000 are the towns and they too can be categorized as large, medium, and small. This kind of categorization provides a sense of the size differences that exist within the urban system of the country. It also enables size-class comparisons of key economic and social indicators which can reveal things both about the populations of the respective settlements as well as their quality of life.

The census definition of 'cities' is quite old dating back to, at least, 1951 when there were fewer large cities and 100,000 was a realistic cut-off for differentiating between towns and cities. But, in the last sixty years, so much has changed. Not only are there many more, large and very large cities, they have also become more complex in structure. Most of the larger urban places have grown in area as well as population and have encompassed neighbouring smaller towns and villages to form urban 'agglomerations'. The latter term, also used by the census, refers to a core town or city surrounded by smaller urban settlements and urban outgrowths. The largest of the urban agglomerations include those of Mumbai, Delhi, Kolkata, Chennai, Bengaluru, and Hyderabad.

Urban agglomerations with a population in excess of 1 million are called metropolitan cities. According to the Census of 2001, there were thirty-five metropolitan cities and together they accounted for 107 million people or 38 per cent of the total urban population. Provisional data from the Census of 2011 indicate that this number has gone up to 53 and that they now contain 42 per cent of the country's urban population. This concentration of the total urban population in the largest cities of the urban system is likely to get even more accentuated in the future. According to the Mckinsey 2010 report on urbanization, India will have 68 cities of more than 1 million people by 2030 and they will account for almost half of the country's total urban population. In light of this urbanization pattern, where there is continuous growth in population at the upper end of the system, a restricted focus, as planned for this book, on the larger urban settlements can be justified. Table 1 presents a state-wise distribution of cities, that is, urban places with a population of 100,000 and above in 2011.

TABLE 1 India 2011—Distribution of Cities by State

State/Union territory	Total number of cities (100,000 and above pop.)	Number of cities (500,000–1 million pop.)	Number of cities (1,000,000 and above pop.)
Jharkhand	10	1	2
Bihar	26	0	1
Andhra Pradesh	42	3	3
West Bengal	61	3	2
Uttar Pradesh	64	9	7
Maharashtra	44	8	10
Punjab	17	1	2
Tamil Nadu	32	2	3
Karnataka	26	3	1

Kerala	7	2	0
Gujarat	30	2	4
Rajasthan	29	2	3
Madhya Pradesh	32	1	4
Haryana	20	1	1
Uttarakhand	6	1	0
Chhattisgarh	9	1	1
Orissa	10	2	0
Jammu and Kashmir	3	1	1
Himachal Pradesh	1	0	0
NCT of Delhi	15	0	1
Chandigarh	1	1	0
Puducherry	2	0	0
Andaman and Nicobar	1	0	0
The North-East			
Sikkim	0	0	0
Assam	4	1	0
Meghalaya	1	0	0
Manipur	1	0	0
Mizoram	1	0	0
Tripura	1	0	0
Nagaland	1	0	0
Arunachal Pradesh	0	0	0

Source: Census of India, Provisional Population Totals, Paper 2 of 2011: India (Vol. II). Available at http://www.censusindia.gov.in/ 2011-prov-results/paper2/prov_results_paper2_indiavol2.html, accessed on 5 January 2012.

As Table 1 shows, Uttar Pradesh has the largest number of cities followed by West Bengal where there are many small cities but few large ones. In contrast, Maharashtra with a smaller total has ten cities with a population of over a million and eight cities with a population between 500,000 and 1 million.

At the other end of the spectrum are the small mountainous states. In 2001, Himachal Pradesh, Sikkim, Arunachal Pradesh, and Nagaland did not have even one city while Manipur, Mizoram, Tripura, and Meghalaya had only one city, the capital city, with a population of above 100,000. But by 2011, the capitals of Nagaland and Himachal Pradesh exceeded this figure.

Figure 1 shows the geographical distribution of urban places with a population of 100,000 and above as of 2001. They have been categorized as follows: those with a population of 1 million and above; those with a population of less than 1 million to 500,000; and those with a population of less than 500,000 to 100,000. The first category is the large city, the second is the medium-sized city, and the third is the small city. Apart from the mountainous north-east and the north-west Himalayan region and the western edge of Rajasthan, the interiors of Orissa and Andhra Pradesh are starkly devoid of cities of any size. However, for the

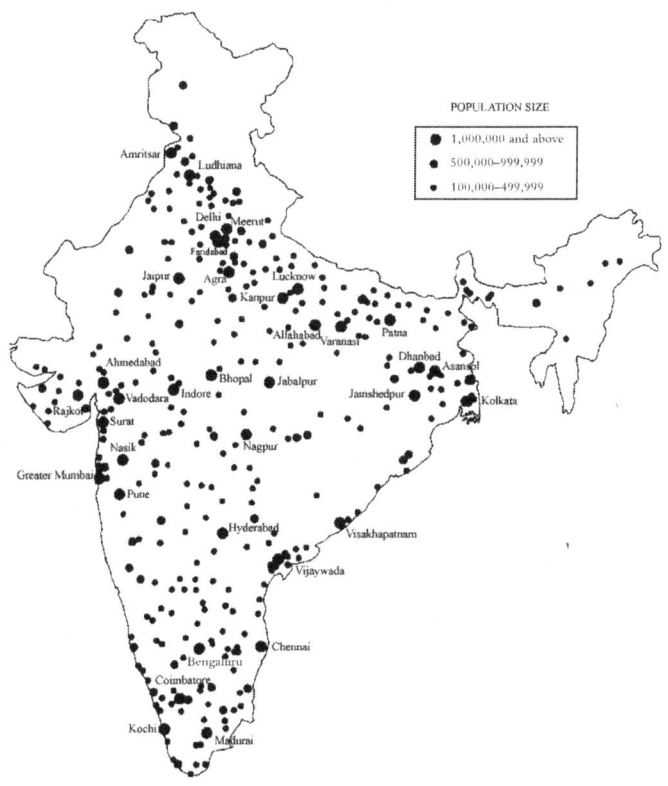

FIGURE 1 Geographical distribution of cities of all sizes in 2001

Source: Based on Census of India, 2001. Series 1: India. Final Population Totals, Urban Agglomerations and Towns.

country as a whole, looking at the distribution of the dots of different sizes, it is evident that there is a good representation of cities throughout its geographical area. The medium and small-sized cities, in particular, could hold the key to balanced national development by their location in all corners of the country.

★ ★ ★

It should be kept in mind that cities are a product of not just more and more population growth around a nucleus of advantage, but also embody practices and understandings of a way of life best suited to prevailing local conditions. These constitute a specific type of urbanism ingrained in building and living practices that influence the form and growth of the city. It is necessary to first turn to the Indian city's historical past in order to uncover some of the characteristics typical of its urbanism and to understand what forces have shaped it.

1

The Indian City in History

The contemporary Indian city is a product of a multi-layered and continuous civilization that goes back into pre-history. This does not mean that the cities of today can be traced back into pre-history. What it does mean is that like Indian civilization itself, Indian cities have over the centuries absorbed influences from diverse sources and, in the cities of today, these can be seen in architectural styles and building form as well as in the relationship between public space and social life.

A historical overview of Indian urbanism necessitates consideration of the numerous cultural influences that have shaped Indian civilization and the multilayered nature of its historical legacy where an internally developed cultural tradition roughly established by 1000 BC was through the centuries modified by external influences. The urban built environment in India has been a product of the assimilation and hybridization of centuries of cultural contact with diverse influences entering the subcontinent via both land and sea routes. It is also a product of the character of the land and its ability to support non-agricultural activities, location vis-à-vis means of communication and trade as well as local and regional political and cultural influences. Trying to throw light on the characteristics of Indian urbanism in such a varied context and stretching across the several millennia that mark this civilization, is too a huge task for the present short format.

Chronologically, we can think of three broad periods which have left their mark on urbanism or the urban way of life in the subcontinent: the pre-colonial, colonial, and postcolonial. A practical way of approaching this vast history is by focusing on state, society, and urban form and seeing in what ways they have changed across these three periods.

The Pre-colonial Period

The Early Period

In ancient India, the formations that approximated the state have generally been regarded as having been of secondary importance or epiphenomenon. An impersonal, often un-institutionalized religious order held together the social practices of society and determined the everyday lives of ordinary people rather than a strong political entity. In fact, while kingdoms and dynasties rose and fell, territorialities based on religion and economics showed greater stability. Thus, during the earliest incidence of urbanism that occurred during the Bronze Age when the Indus valley or Harappan civilization reached its maturity around 2500 BC to 1900 BC, cities were not necessarily tied to political territories or guided by strong political leaders. Urbanism occurred in the absence of a strong centralized state with early cities emerging as centres of social and economic networks that remained stable in politically fragmented landscapes and in which urbanism was not always connected to territorial political activities.

The Harappan civilization was based on a network of towns and cities that flourished along the Indus valley and one of its main characteristics was planning of a truly amazing nature. The straight streets meeting at right angles, a superb drainage system for carrying away rainwater, cesspools for clearing sewage, the large-scale public architecture, the high level of urban organization and the numerous seals with Indus script indicate the presence of a supra-household authority that coordinated these activities. But there is no evidence of a single dominant hierarchy within the cities and the settlements are better perceived to have been clustered cities with a balance of authority among groups. To this decentralized model of authority must be added that fact that the cities were not built for military activities and the Indus culture lacked an iconography of warfare or dominance. Rather, its leaders, religious or secular, were more focused on ritual performance, economic activities, and urban cohesion. For ordinary people, the cities provided more secure food supplies and a large variety of goods and attractions beyond mere survival such as styles of pottery and bangles not found in the hinterland.

Distinctions in craft production techniques have led to the suggestion that producer groups may have had different ethnicities or that workshops were producing for different clienteles. While definitive evidence is awaited, the existing information suffices for us to conclude that a robust urbanism existed over the western part of the subcontinent during the Bronze Age with well-planned and managed settlements that catered to a socially and economically diverse population.

The next phase of urbanism occurred more than a thousand years later starting around 500 BC in the Ganga Valley and lasting till AD 300 and is associated with well-known towns such as Rajagriha, Ayodhya, Kashi, Vaishali, Ujjain, and Taxila. They were ruled by different kings and apart from the brief period of the Mauryas covering 321 BC to 185 BC, this was a time when the subcontinent was characterized by numerous republics and kingdoms. In all, around 60 simultaneously occupied urban settlements of 50–300 hectares have been identified with this period but there is not much evidence of how and when these population centres first came into existence. They probably grew around what had been villages that had specialized in particular crafts and trading centres as specialized craft workers tended to congregate in such places. Most towns had ramparts and fortified walls. Internally there was differentiation by guilds with each guild occupying a particular section of the town.

There was some form of town-planning and several types of town plans have been identified. Most towns were walled with two wide main streets cutting across at right angles to each other. The rest of the street system comprised narrow and irregular roads with the palace, fort, or temple forming the core area.

In the south of the subcontinent, urban settlements such as at Kotalingala, Dhulikatta, Peddabankur, and Konadpur in the central Deccan flourished during the period 300 BC to AD 200. Their structural remains, though far from uniform, reveal the existence of planned layouts, mud fortifications, palace complexes, granaries, and provision for water storage and cisterns. Despite their geographical proximity, the settlements reveal an overall pattern distinct from each other and so probably they were not under a common administrative authority that could enforce uniform or identical layout plans or architectural forms. In summary, like the earliest period of Indian urbanism, this period too was characterized by decentralized authority and diversity in residents. The exception was, of course, the period of the Mauryan Empire (321 BC–AD 185) when almost the entire subcontinent was under one ruler.

Textual sources indicate that apart from kings and rulers, there were other groups with financial and social authority. These included corporate groups such as guilds and traders' groups who together with landowners, nuns, and monks made donations to religious institutions. Kings and rulers were thus not the only sponsors of ritual activity and neither did they have complete control over economic activities. The existence of countervailing sources of financial and social authority within the society of early historic India enabled much more local control and this became evident during the Gupta period (AD 300–AD 700) when the administration of each city was through a council which consisted of the president of the city corporation, the chief representative of the guild merchants, a representative of the artisans, and the chief scribe. These councils may have been duplicated for each ward of the city and they consisted of local representatives rather than state appointees.

The early historic period of urban growth was followed by the period AD 800–1200 when power shifted to the landowning community, and towns and urban centres and the urban guilds lost their dominant positions in the northern half of the subcontinent. But after AD 1200 towns began to flourish once more and this continued for several centuries. In fact, the period of the Mughul Empire or the sixteenth, seventeenth, and part of the eighteenth century, appears to have been the 'veritable golden age of urbanization' for much of northern and central India. There was both an expansion of pre-existing towns and cities as well as a proliferation of new ones. Thus this period deserves closer attention.

The Mughal Period

In contrast to the earliest period and the early historical period, from the medieval period, the prosperity of urban centres over the subcontinent began to depend more and more on political conditions favourable to the pursuit of urban trades and crafts. During the reigns of Akbar, Jahangir and Shahjahan, and for much of the reign of Aurangzeb, an urban-based economy and urban culture flourished due to the establishment of political conditions that facilitated commerce and were advantageous to the trading and artisan classes of the cities. However, it is difficult to point out a typical Indian city of this period given the profound differences between northern and southern cities, coastal and interior cities, and Hindu and Indo-Islamic cities.

Several northern cities such as Delhi and Agra and western cities such as Ahmedabad and Surat were of the latter type. Their partially Islamic character is seen in their physical appearance, their layout, and the distribution of non-residential space. Typical features included palace-forts often reflecting military architecture of non-Indian origin, open areas (*maidans*) for military parades and equestrian exercises, religious structures such as mosques, tombs and colleges, bazaars and caravan serai, and massive walls and gateways. The larger cities tended to spill out beyond the walls and display some amount of urban sprawl.

As in the earlier periods, towns and cities did not have any kind of corporate or municipal institution and most urban communities in Mughal India were largely self-regulating, if not self-governing in regard to the provision of basic services. Every city or town was divided into wards or *mohalla*s which had a self-regulatory role. The mohallas were based on occupation or caste or ethnicity and religion or through the sharing of some kind of organic identity through migration from the same village or region. Their group identity was further reinforced by walls separating them from adjacent mohallas with gates that were closed at night and at times of unrest. Mohallas would have been able to provide some of the basic needs of their inhabitants as well as justice through arbitration by a panchayat or a respected elder.

The Mughal state's presence in city or town affairs was made felt via the *kotwal* or prefect of police who was provided with a staff and a large number of armed soldiers to maintain law and order, apprehend and punish criminals, assess and collect taxes within the city proper, enforce regulations governing the operation of city markets, and act as moral police. The kotwal's authority was very extensive and if he and his subordinates were diligent in their duties, the towns and cities of Mughal India would have been very strictly controlled on behalf of the central government. But, in reality, this was rarely so.

In southern India, there were broadly three elements which accounted for the significant urbanization noted during medieval times. They included the presence of temples, administrative functions including military ones and markets, and handicraft production. But the mix of these three elements varied giving rise to different kinds of towns. One distinct presence in the urban landscape was the *gopuram* or temple gateway. The temple complexes of the late medieval period were great walled places with towering gateways and in their internal structure they had the appearance of being highly fortified. Eighteenth-century plans for several such cities show that they generally contained more than one temple, markets, palaces, women's quarters, quarters for soldiers and their horses, as well as residential spaces for town inhabitants.

To summarize, in pre-colonial times, a self-regulatory, non-codified, and localized means of urban control largely prevailed. Growth of the city through additions or extensions to existing houses or through the construction of new structures was on the basis of informal agreement between immediate neighbours rather than via a centralized authority. Local control is also seen in the fact that the state was not the universal arbitrator or dispenser of justice and basically confined itself to taxing subjects and policing infringements of caste practices. On the economic front, trade and commerce, both within the country and outside, were organized by private merchants with state support and were vital triggers for the growth and sustenance of an urban culture both during ancient India and medieval times.

Urbanism of the pre-colonial period has left its own legacy to the Indian city of contemporary times.

In material form, this legacy is today best seen in the walled sections of old cities such as Ahmedabad and Delhi and in the layout of the original core of old towns and cities throughout India, and also in the remnants of the native or indigenous quarters or the 'Black Town' sections of the biggest cities. These historic districts contain traditional types of housing, street layout, livelihood patterns, and an old-world way of life. They support very high population densities and a variety of economic activities. There is still much to learn from them.

The Colonial Period

The colonial period which lasted two hundred years saw the introduction of many rules, regulations, and practices that aimed to make Indian cities more easily manageable and legible to the British so that control over them would be easier. Serious attempts to change the character of Indian cities date to the aftermath of the 1857 uprising when cities such as Delhi and Lucknow witnessed widening of streets, demolition of crowded areas, and the establishment of physical markers of the imperial colonial presence.

Takeover of land and property from those suspected to have been involved in the 1857 uprising by the colonial state provided the means to restructure the core of the old city of Delhi and to change its social and economic composition. Simultaneously, north of the old city, a new settlement for the British and their army was created and the nucleus of a dualistic city thereby established where civil lines and cantonment marked a distinct area from the old indigenous city. New rules and regulations for the management of the city were also introduced via the establishment of a nominated municipal authority with fines and fees instituted for various activities such as the extension of existing buildings that, prior to this, city dwellers had undertaken in an ad hoc and informal way. Pre-existing systems of water supply and solid waste collection were bypassed for more modern systems that over the years created problems of their own. The colonial state's interest in collecting maximum taxes and being financially strong underlay many of its concerns about the need for the expansion of the city and the construction of new residential layouts for the better off.

The resident population was not a passive spectator to these changes but responded in multiple ways of which building or extending built-up area without permission was one of the most frequent. These illegal structures were usually regularized with the payment of a fine. Other responses are to be seen in the way indigenous buildings changed in design and layout absorbing some of the new influences in unique ways that highlighted the existence of the process of 'indigenous modernity'. In the indigenous or Indian portions of the colonial city, houses and building styles began to reflect colonial influences not in their pure forms but adapted to suit the local vernacular.

Overall, the impact of the colonial period on urbanism in the subcontinent was profound and marks a distinct break with the past. The first was through the introduction of new settlement forms such as the civil station and the cantonment which radically changed the structure of the traditional town or city in India from a compact one centred around a single core to a more extended structure wherein the civil lines and cantonment developed as suburbs outside the old core. While the civil lines contained the administrative offices, courts, as well as the residences of the officers, the cantonment housed the military. Built in a planned way at very low density and with large open spaces, they were a physical contrast to the 'native' town. With sharp inequalities in the levels of basic amenities between the anglicized additions and the old parts, they heralded the origins of today's dual-city phenomena. It was primarily in the administrative centres of the British Raj that the civil lines were created, that is, in the provincial capitals, the district headquarters, and the *tehsil*-level administrative centres. The cantonment, on the other hand, was built only near major towns and in all there were about 114 of them, mostly in the plains of Punjab and western Uttar Pradesh for reasons of security. Other pre-existing towns, not of administrative or military importance, were ignored.

Second, the construction of public buildings in European architectural styles and their arrangement in physical space to display the power and might of the Raj resulted in startling contrasts with indigenous forms further highlighting the slowly emerging urban dualities. Third, the colonial period also saw the establishment of many new towns and cities which were very different from indigenous towns. These varied in scale from the small hill stations and canal colony towns to the metropolitan port cities of Mumbai, Kolkata, and Chennai. Fourth, colonialism was the medium by which industrial capitalism was introduced into India and along with it came new forms of technology and organization such as the railways, ports, factories, and warehouses. The networks of transportation and the institutional buildings associated with these new forms of activities were to completely transform portions of existing cities. It was also to alter the occupational structure of the urban workforce, bringing in factory workers and mill hands from rural areas into large cities, such as Mumbai, Kolkata, Bengaluru, and Chennai, and changing their social and economic composition.

Finally, ideas of modernity embodied in Western education and Western law were to have profound effects on local elites. For the working class too, employed in the new factories and offices relatively unhindered by the kinds of sanctions based on caste and religion that rural areas imposed, there was a sense of freedom in the anonymity of the large seething metropolis and also the hope of a better future. Thus British colonialism was the harbinger of modernity in Indian society but it was a 'divided modernity' experienced differently by the elites and the poor or the subalterns. This division was directly reflected in their residences—where the rich and poor lived in the city and how they lived. The civil lines and their extensions were always well maintained and well serviced as contrasted to the indigenous portions of the city where the poor and migrant workers lived in crowded tenements close to their workplaces.

The Post-independence Period till 1991

With independence in 1947, urbanization rapidly speeded up for a number of reasons. In the immediate aftermath of Indian independence on 15 August 1947 refugees from the newly created nation of Pakistan poured into the Punjab and along the eastern border into Bengal. Many, particularly those on the western border, headed for urban areas, and so there was an immediate need to create urban housing on a large scale to accommodate them. Around 7.3 million refugees were registered in 1951 and while towns such as Jullunder, Ludhiana, Amritsar, and Ambala in the Punjab, Kolkata in the east, and the national capital, Delhi, were enlarged through the development of new colonies or suburbs to accommodate them, it was clearly not enough. In all about 14 new towns had to be built and these 14 towns built between 1947 and

1951, were scattered over eight major states. By 1951 they accommodated 470,000 refugees.

According to the Indian census, between 1941 and 1951, the population of India's cities grew by 41 per cent and the war together with the famine of 1942 hastened the movement of people to cities. Between 1951 and 1961, there was a 26 per cent increase in urban population with 18 per cent of India's total population residing in urban areas. Moreover, the process of reorganization of the states within India after 1956 led to the creation of several new states which required new capitals and administrative centres. Thus demographic, economic, and administrative factors all played a role in accelerating the rate of urbanization and the need for the building of new towns, which became a major feature of the urban history of this period.

By 1971, 112 new towns had been built, a large number of them during the 1950s up to the mid-1960s coinciding with the period of India's early and rapid industrialization. Apart from state capitals such as Chandigarh, Bhubaneswar, and Gandhinagar, the development of many of the new towns was linked to the location of heavy industries and power projects, for instance, Bhailainagar–Drug, Bokaro, Durgapur, and Rourkela. A few such as Kalayni in the Kolkata metropolitan area were created to take care of population growth in the core city. Except for a few company towns such as Modinagar and Jamshedpur, the new towns were generally financed and built by the state.

The building of the new towns met several needs, from providing jobs and homes for refugees and absorbing excess population from the older urban areas, to generating economic development in the local region and serving as symbols of the new, modern India that was emerging. The new town that best represented these multiple concerns was Chandigarh, in Punjab, the genesis of which dates back to the immediate aftermath of the Partition in 1947. The building of Chandigarh came to symbolize not just the recovery of the Punjab after the Partition, but also the regeneration of the whole nation. It was Nehru's dream project to chart a new modern India.

The economic foundations of the new republic of India were laid in the early Five Year Plans which also saw considerable state involvement in urban policy and planning. During the period of the first two Five Year Plans (1951–6, 1956–61) several important institutions for urban administration and for the training of skilled professionals were created by the central government. These included a Ministry of Urban Affairs, the National Buildings Organization, . the School of Planning and Architecture in New Delhi, a Regional and Town Planning Department in the Indian Institute of Technology Kharagpur, and the Town and Country Planning Organization, the technical unit of the Ministry of Urban Affairs. The latter organization prepared the Master Plan for Delhi in 1957 and also model legislation for town planning to be enacted by state governments. During the 1960s, several states enacted such legislation and created town planning departments which, with the help of central grants, prepared over 500 master plans for individual cities.

But with the rapid urbanization that followed independence and a threefold increase in urban population from 62 million in 1951 to 159 million in 1981 to 217 million in 1991, these plans were thrown into disarray. They have remained mostly on paper.

Another discernible characteristic of urbanization throughout much of the last century has been the faster growth of large towns and cities with the result that there has been an increasing concentration of urban population in such settlements. At the same time, since 1901, small towns have lost population. This is strikingly illustrated in Table 2 which shows comparable data for the late colonial period 1901–41 and the nationalist period 1951–91.

TABLE 2 Percentage of Urban Population Living in Towns of Various Sizes

Census year	100,000 and above	99,999– 50,000	49,999– 20,000	< 20,000
1901	26.00	11.29	15.64	47.07
1941	38.23	11.42	16.35	34.00
1951	44.63	9.96	15.72	29.69
1991	64.89	10.96	13.33	10.82

Source: Sivaramakrishnan et al. (2005: 38, Table 3.5).

At the beginning of the last century, small towns of less than 20,000 people were the predominant kind of town and accounted for nearly half or 47 per cent of India's total urban population. By 1991, this had fallen to just 11 per cent while towns with a population of 100,000 and above, called Class I towns, accounted for 65 per cent of the total urban population. The number of Class I towns also increased significantly from 24 in 1901 to 76 in 1951 to 300 in 1991.

An associated development has been that of metropolization, which refers to the rapid increase in numbers of very large or metropolitan cities. In India, the term metropolitan city is used for those settlements that have a population of 1 million and above. In 1901, there was just one such city, namely, Kolkata. By 1951, this had increased to four, that is, Kolkata, Mumbai, Chennai, and Delhi. By 1981, the number of such cities had increased to twelve and by 1991 to twenty-three. These large, sprawling cities have remained the economic magnets of the country drawing more and more people with the promise of jobs and a better life.

In the early decades after independence, a wide range of manufacturing jobs supported a considerable proportion of the working population in large cities. But with the decline of old industries such as jute manufacturing since the 1960s and cotton textiles since the 1980s, city economies tied to these industries were unable to remain dynamic unless they became export-oriented or diversified into newer sectors. The economic structure of the largest cities began to reflect this reality with a significant fall in manufacturing activity for both men and women and a simultaneous increase in service sector jobs. Between 1981 and 1991, the numbers of factory workers in Mumbai declined from 604,000 to 447,000 while Ahmedabad lost 50,000 mill jobs between 1983–4 and 1995. Aggregate data on urban areas as a whole indicate a gradual decline in the percentage of male workers (usual status) engaged in manufacturing from 27 per cent in 1983 to around 24 per cent in 1993–4. For female workers (usual status) the decline was from 26 per cent in 1983 to 24 per cent in 1993–4. Over the same period, while the percentage of male workers engaged in services increased from 25 to 26 per cent, the increase in women workers was from 31 to 38 per cent. This is illustrated with data for one city, Mumbai, as shown in Table 3.

The decline of the blue-collar industry in the core of the city was accompanied by a decline in population as well, but losses in jobs and population by the core were largely offset by an increase in both on the metropolitan fringes. Mumbai is perhaps the best example of this process of decentralization. In 1961, the core of the city (Bombay Island) had a population of 2.7 million which was two-thirds of Greater Mumbai's total population. In 1991, Bombay Island's population of 3.3 million was only 33 per cent of the Greater Mumbai total of 9.9

TABLE 3   Change in Economic Activities in Greater Mumbai, 1971–91

Greater Mumbai Municipal Corporation economic activities	1971 employment (%)	1991 employment (%)
Manufacturing	44.1	28.5
Trade	18.6	29.1
Transport	8.4	5.4
Services and finance	26.9	34.1
Other	2.0	2.9
Total	100.0	100.0

Source: Greater Mumbai Economic Census, 1971 and 1991, cited from Sita and Bhagat (2007: 75).

million. Similarly, the population of the area within the jurisdiction of the Kolkata Municipal Corporation (KMC) was growing slowly in relation to that of the Calcutta Urban Agglomeration which is made up of a string of towns extending from the city and located on both sides of the Hugli River. In 1991, with 4.4 million people, the KMC accounted for just around 40 per cent of the urban agglomeration's total population.

Despite the gradual slowdown in manufacturing employment, overall, for all the decades covering the nationalist period, that is 1951–91, other than 1961, the growth rate of the urban population exceeded

3 per cent per annum. This brought along the attendant problems of over-stretched housing and basic infrastructure. Unable to afford available legal accommodation, the poor in the city settled down on open spaces, wherever available and built their own makeshift housing. To earn a living they turned to the informal sector. By 1991, the informal sector accounted for 66 per cent of the jobs in Mumbai and 55 per cent in Kolkata. Thus a concomitant feature of urbanization in the post-independence period has been the growth of slums and squatter settlements in Indian cities and along with this a growing informal sector.

Inevitably, the city had to expand laterally to accommodate the increasing numbers and this happened through the development of planned suburbs and satellite towns as well as through unplanned and haphazard growth along the peripheries of the city. At the same time, the sharp differences between the civil lines and the remainder of the city have slowly got obliterated with the political amalgamation of the Raj enclaves into the city. But a new kind of dualism, that between the slums and non-slum areas of the city, became an entrenched feature of the postcolonial city. By 1991, 21 per cent of India's urban population was residing in slums. It was much higher in large cities such as Mumbai where this figure was 43 per cent, in Kolkata 36 per cent, and in Delhi 22 per cent.

★ ★ ★

The Indian city in the post-independence period up to 1991 was thus already a city of considerable contrasts with an old elite, both propertied and industrial, that remained cocooned in the privileges of the Raj days and its associated lifestyle, an emerging middle class comprising those with a firm base in government jobs and the security of public sector housing, as well as small business owners and traders, a declining formal working class with jobs in the organized manufacturing sector, and increasing numbers of the poor eking out a living mostly in various kinds of services in the ubiquitous informal sector. This then was the context within which the Indian economy was opened up in 1991. Its effects on the city are discussed in the following chapters.

2

Urban Growth in the Post-liberalization Era

Urban growth in the post-liberalization era has been marked by both continuities with the past as well as discontinuities. Continuities are best seen in the broader process of urbanization, which has been characterized by the same features as noted in the last chapter, namely, the faster growth of larger towns, metropolization, decline of manufacturing jobs, spreading outwards of the city, and growth of slums and squatter settlements. The discontinuities are unfolding gradually and require more careful analysis.

It has been 20 years since the opening up of the Indian economy in 1991 and its impact on Indian cities, hardly noticeable after the first decade, has since the second decade emerged as striking and significant in certain parts of the city. The changes are an ongoing process heralding even greater transformations to come. They have been driven partly by the needs of the growing cities themselves as the country enters its third decade of fairly high economic growth and partly by changes in macro-economic policy and India's position in global markets.

Since 2000, the country's seven largest cities, each with a population exceeding 4 million, have been experiencing a construction boom from rapidly growing residential and office real estate as well as from large infrastructure projects such as flyovers, the creation and extension of metro systems, circular rail systems, airports, high-speed road connectors, shopping malls, and entertainment centres. In the process, considerable land use change has been occurring and the look and feel of certain parts of the cities is palpably different. In smaller cities, the change is mostly confined to residential and office real estate and shopping malls.

Forces Driving City Growth

What are the forces driving the growth of India's cities in the post-liberalization period? They are both local and global. In the popular media, there has been a tendency to connect all forms of change in the economy, society, and culture to globalization. In reality, much of the change is being driven by the needs of the internal economy and one of the main drivers is demographics or the rate of growth of population in these cities. This is a local force. Table 4 shows the decennial growth rates of the thirty-five cities or urban agglomerations with a population of 1 million and above in 2001. The term urban agglomeration includes the core city and its surrounding suburbs and outgrowths. If these growth rates are seen against the decennial growth rate of 31.3 per cent during 1991–2001 for urban India as a whole, then it becomes clear that two-thirds of these agglomerations have been growing at higher rates than the national average. Only twelve of the thirty-five urban agglomerations had a growth rate less than the national average. However what Table 4 also makes clear is that the suburbs and peripheral areas of the large Indian city are growing faster than the inner core area. As mentioned in Chapter 1, this process which has resulted in considerable decentralization of both people and jobs predates economic liberalization and was seen in the 1991 census data. In older metropolitan cities such as Kolkata, Chennai, Hyderabad, Ahmedabad, Coimbatore, Vadodara, Kochi, and Varanasi, growth in the city proper has further slowed down between 1991 and 2001 while for the city of Madurai, it has been negative. The latest data, provisional results of the 2011 census, indicate a continuation of the slow growth or negative growth trend of the core areas of several large cities. Exceptions to this trend have been Bengaluru, Meerut, Nashik, Asansol, and Rajkot, the last four being relatively small metropolitan cities.

TABLE 4 Decennial Growth Rate of India's 35 Cities/Urban Agglomerations with Million Plus Population, 1981–91 and 1991–2001

Cities/UA	Pop.	UA growth		Core city growth	
	2001	1981–91	1991–2001	1981–91	1991–2001
1. Greater Mumbai	16.36	33.7	29.9	20.4	20.4
2. Kolkata	13.21	19.9	19.9	6.6	4.1
3. Delhi	12.79	46.9	51.9	43.2	36.2
4. Chennai	6.42	26.4	18.5	28.9	9.7
5. Bengaluru	5.68	41.3	37.8	7.4	61.3
6. Hyderabad	5.53	66.6	27.4	39.2	12.8
7. Ahmedabad	4.51	29.5	36.4	22.9	18.9
8. Pune	3.75	44.8	50.6	30.2	38.3
9. Surat	2.81	64.4	85.1	62.2	62.3
10. Kanpur	2.69	23.8	32.5	25.8	35.0

11. Jaipur	2.32	49.6	53.1	49.2	59.4
12. Lucknow	2.26	65.7	35.8	70.8	36.3
13. Nagpur	2.12	36.4	27.6	33.2	26.2
14. Patna	1.70	19.7	55.3	18.1	33.4
15. Indore	1.63	33.7	47.8	31.6	46.3
16. Vadodara	1.49	44.0	32.4	40.4	26.6
17. Bhopal	1.45	58.4	36.9	8.3	34.9
18. Coimbatore	1.44	19.6	31.4	15.9	13.1
19. Ludhiana	1.39	71.8	33.7	71.7	33.7
20. Kochi	1.35	38.3	18.8	13.5	2.4
21. Visakhapatnam	1.33	75.1	25.7	33.0	28.9
22. Agra	1.32	26.9	39.4	28.5	29.2
23. Varanasi	1.21	29.3	17.5	29.6	18.4
24. Madurai	1.19	19.7	10.0	14.6	−1.9
25. Meerut	1.16	56.5	37.4	76.9	42.5
26. Nashik	1.15	63.7	58.8	80.6	63.9
27. Jabalpur	1.11	17.4	25.7	20.8	22.0
28. Jamshedpur	1.10	21.9	32.9	5.1	23.8
29. Asansol	1.09	52.0	42.7	42.9	85.4
30. Dhanbad	1.06	18.9	30.5	26.2	31.1
31. Faridabad	1.05	86.7	70.8	86.7	70.8
32. Allahabad	1.04	29.9	4.3	28.7	24.9
33. Amritsar	1.01	19.2	42.6	19.2	27.3
34. Vijaywada	1.01	37.8	19.6	32.9	17.6
35. Rajkot	1.00	47.1	53.1	25.7	72.8

Source: Census of India, 2001 and Sita and Bhagat (2007).
Note: All-India urban decennial growth rate was 36.10 per cent for 1981–91 and 31.30 per cent for 1991–2001.
UA—urban agglomeration.

Growing population, particularly in the suburbs and peripheral areas of the largest urban agglomerations has had a direct impact on the demand for goods and services and has led to further extensions of the city. Spreading outwards to meet the rising demand for housing, office space, schools, hospitals, and other services, Indian cities are swallowing up smaller towns and villages surrounding their periphery. We see this in the increasing merger of smaller towns or their inclusion in the larger urban agglomeration. Between 1991 and 2001, 221 towns were thus merged, a number that is twice that for the 1981–91 decade.

Expectations of a significant increase in the urban population by 2030 have also become the concern of the central government, which in 2005 introduced a new programme, the JNNURM (Jawaharlal Nehru National Urban Renewal Mission), to upgrade and extend urban infrastructure in the largest cities of the country. Reports in the media of how large cities need a complete makeover if they are to meet the challenges of the twenty-first century have re-enforced the concerns of policymakers. Thus demographics, both of the present and the future, are an important driver of the attempts by Indian cities to augment their infrastructure and restructure their land uses.

Global influences on the growth of Indian cities are more difficult to isolate although much of the improved economic performance of the country since 1991 has been attributed to the opening up of the economy. In the first decade, 1991–2001, opening up necessitated deregulation of the industrial sector and streamlining of the financial sector. These being urban-based activities, the first decade of reforms mainly benefitted urban areas of the country. Several metropolitan regions became increasingly attractive for the setting up of new economy industries. Global influence on the local can be seen in the presence of foreign direct investment (FDI) in such industries. It can also be seen in the office space required by numerous business process outsourcing (BPO) and knowledge process out sourcing (KPO) industries springing up in the larger cities. In addition, there is the direct impact on the built environment through increasing use of global expertise in the planning and design of information technology parks and BPO workspaces, upmarket real estate projects, and commercial properties. Though these projects have been built locally and with local materials, there is a strong global element in their conception, design, and subsequent usage.

Economically Dynamic Urban Corridors and Clusters of Cities

An important aspect of post-liberalization urban growth has been a sharper differentiation between urban areas in terms of their suitability for investment and the creation of new industries. The old hierarchy of the four mega-cities, namely, Mumbai, Kolkata, Chennai, and Delhi dominating the western, eastern, southern, and northern regions, has given way to urban corridors and clusters of new investment around smaller metropolitan cities located mostly in the southern and western parts of the country as shown in Figure 2.

The Delhi region and adjacent areas in Haryana, Punjab, Rajasthan, and Uttar Pradesh (UP) form another high-investment zone. Other than this, much of the north, east, and centre of the country has been, so far, bypassed. A vast area covering the eastern half of UP and stretching across Bihar, West Bengal, Orissa, the newly created states of Jharkhand and Chhattisgarh, Madhya Pradesh, and the eastern half of Maharashtra remain locked in old industrial bases and high unemployment. They have become the 'sending

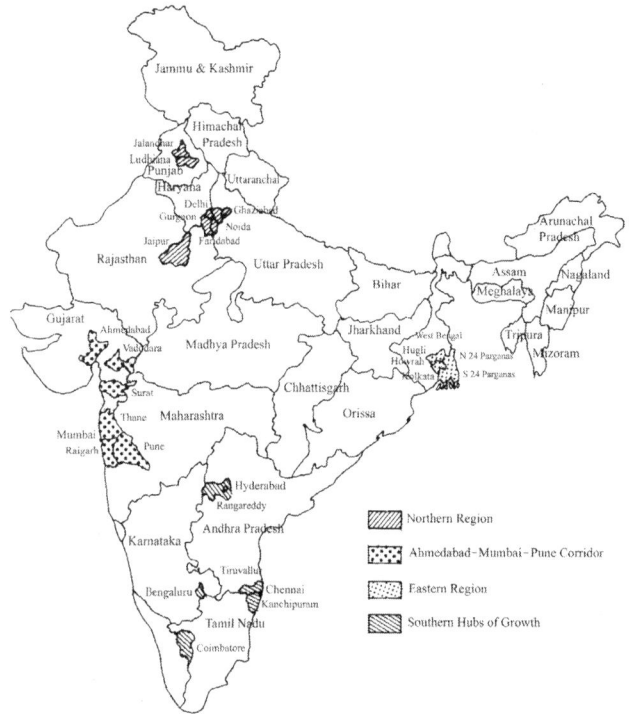

FIGURE 2   Urban corridors and clusters, 2001
Source: Based on Census of India, 2001. Series 1: India. Final
Population Totals, Urban Agglomerations and Towns.

out' areas of skilled and unskilled labour to the economically dynamic urban regions of the country.

Both the quantity and type of investment coming
into the different urban regions are interesting to note

and details on these are provided by the Centre for Monitoring the Indian Economy (CMIE), an autonomous statistical organization based in Mumbai which has been publishing data on various aspects of investment in India since 1995. The data are disaggregated by state and district and since some of the largest cities are coextensive with entire districts, it is possible to discern the investment coming into these cities. The cumulative investment in large projects, that is, of Rs 1 crore (10 million) and above, received by the major cities and their adjoining districts between June 1995 and December 2010 is shown in Table 5.

From Table 5, it is clear that the Ahmedabad–Mumbai–Pune urban corridor has been the largest investment destination with Mumbai and the adjoining districts of Thane and Raigarh receiving a little above a million crores. Similarly, Delhi and its adjoining districts of Faridabad, Gurgaon, Ghaziabad, and Noida have received over a million crores. In both Delhi and Mumbai, the adjoining areas have received more investment than the city itself. In contrast, in the south, that is, in Chennai, Bengaluru, and Hyderabad, the city proper has received more investments than the adjoining districts. Several smaller metropolises such

TABLE 5 Cumulative Investment in the Dynamic Urban Regions, 1995–2010

UA/Corridor	Investment (Rs crore)	Adjoining districts	Investment (Rs crore)	Total investment (Rs crore)
Western region				
Ahmedabad–Mumbai–Pune corridor				**2,018,266**
Ahmedabad	335,060			335,060
Surat	289,641			289,641
Vadodara	99,091			99,091
Mumbai	500,459	Thane, Raigarh	522,806	1,023,265
Pune	271,209			271,209
Southern hubs of growth				**1,701,658**
Chennai	289,641	Tiruvallur and Kanchipuram	233018	522,659
Bengaluru	345,583	Bengaluru Rural	48,283	393,866
Hyderabad	266,991	Rangareddy	103,108	370,099
Vishakhapatnam	248,773			248,773
Kochi (Ernakulam)	121,990			121,990
Coimbatore	44,271			44,271

(contd...)

Table 5 (*contd...*)

UA/Corridor	Investment (Rs crore)	Adjoining districts	Investment (Rs crore)	Total investment (Rs crore)
Northern region				**1,337,446**
Delhi	378,409	Faridabad, Gurgaon, Ghaziabad, and Noida	682,185	1,060,234
Ludhiana and Jalandhar	100,598			100,598
Jaipur	128,796			128,796
Chandigarh	47,818			47,818

Source: CMIE, CapEx database, accessed in May–June 2011.

as Pune, Surat, Vishakhapatnam, and Kochi have also received fairly large investments and are experiencing dynamic growth. Overall, the quantities of investment received by the economically dynamic regions are in sharp contrast to other urban regions in the country. Their situation is shown in Table 6.

Apart from the Kolkata Urban Agglomeration which includes forty smaller cities and towns and spills over into the adjoining districts of North and South 24 Parganas, Hoogly, and Howrah, cumulative investment in cities outside the economically dynamic parts of the country has been much lower in scale. The Kolkata urban region too has not done all that well. Though much larger in population, it ranks behind smaller metropolitan cities such as Bengaluru, Hyderabad, and Ahmedabad in terms of quantity of investments received.

Urban Investment Patterns

The next interesting question is regarding the sources of investment in urban India. Have the investments mainly come from public or private sources and has FDI been of any significant size in Indian cities?

TABLE 6 Cumulative Investment in Other Urban Regions, 1995–2010

UA	Investment (Rs crore)	Adjoining districts	Investment (Rs crore)	Total (Rs crore)
Eastern region				**483,697**
Kolkata	181,470	N 24 Parganas, S 24 Parganas, Howrah, Hoogly	136,709	318,179
Patna	67,041			67,041
Dhanbad	98,477			98,477
North-central region				**117,882**
Varanasi	18,857			18,857
Lucknow	75,128			75,128
Kanpur	23,897			23,897
Central region				**206,517**
Bhopal	69,326			69,326
Indore	46,521			46,521
Nagpur	90,670			90,670

Source: CMIE, CapEx database.

The cumulative data for the period 1995–2010 indicate a distinct pattern for the core areas of India's major cities and their surrounding urban regions as shown in Table 7.

In the core areas of several major cities, comprising the old municipal corporation areas, there has been significant public investment, the highest being in the capital city of Delhi where central and state government investments together amount to 60 per cent of the total. However, in Kolkata, Chennai, Hyderabad, and Ahmedabad private investment from domestic sources has exceeded public investment. Urban regions surrounding the core city have seen much less public investment and received mostly domestic private investment. This pattern however, is not true for Bengaluru and Hyderabad where the surrounding district has seen substantial state government investment.

What the table shows, very clearly, is that FDI has not been a major contributor to urban projects in the last fifteen years, being, at its highest, only around 16 per cent. Second, most of the FDI has gone to the urban regions of major cities, for instance, suburbs of Bengaluru, rather than the old core areas.

TABLE 7 Sources of Investment in Major Cities and Their Urban Regions, 1995–2010

City/Districts	Location	% central government	% state government	% joint sector	% private (Indian)	% private (foreign)	% other
Mumbai	Core city	21.27	36.62	0.09	36.30	0.72	5.00
Raigad and Thane	Urban region	15.20	12.56	0.29	60.65	10.74	0.56
Kolkata	Core city	27.94	14.52	0.08	52.32	3.06	2.08
Howrah, Hoogly, and 24 Parganas	Urban region	11.20	8.56	0	73.97	4.90	1.38
Delhi	Core city	33.68	26.77	0.00	34.94	1.24	3.37
Faridabad, Gurgaon, Ghaziabad, Noida	Urban region	11.11	6.95	0.00	75.04	6.89	0.01
Chennai	Core city	12.79	25.44	0.36	51.69	7.09	2.63
Tiruvallur and Kanchipuram	Urban region	30.90	14.50	0.68	39.66	13.62	0.65
Bengaluru	Core city	9.56	36.58	0.22	43.57	7.17	2.90
Bengaluru Rural	Urban region	0.18	65.41	0.00	17.91	16.37	0.14
Hyderabad	Core city	5.44	9.04	0.01	76.87	7.61	1.03
Rangareddy	Urban region	4.40	46.05	0.0	45.59	0.56	3.39
Ahmedabad	Core city	15.68	11.32	0.00	62.38	9.57	1.06

Source: CMIE, CapEx database.

What about the smaller metropolitan areas? Who has invested in these cities? To answer these questions, their investment sources are indicated in Table 8.

The smaller metros have been placed region-wise and the key column to note is the fifth one which shows the percentage share of private domestic investment to total investment. This has been low in the metropolitan cities of the central region and north central region, barring Lucknow, the capital of Uttar Pradesh. On the other hand, it has been very high in the northern and western region. Overall, in the smaller metros, investment by the government has been very important, overshadowing private investment. Surat, Pune, and Coimbatore have seen some FDI but, in general, in the smaller metros, its presence is still weak.

Investment by Type of Industry

Economic liberalization in 1991 gave a big boost to new economy industries, several of which are in the service sector. What kinds of investment have actually entered the cities can be discerned from CMIE data on types of projects that have seen investment in various major cities for the period 1995 till 2010. Table 9

TABLE 8 Sources of Investment in Smaller Metropolitan Cities, 1995–2010

City/districts	% central government	% state government	% joint sector	% private (Indian)	% private (foreign)	% other
Western region						
Surat	12.79	25.44	0.36	51.69	7.09	2.63
Vadodara	55.07	5.97	3.08	32.35	3.05	0.48
Pune	19.87	13.07	0.00	56.34	8.98	1.74
Southern region						
Coimbatore	35.60	5.07	2.43	48.82	6.64	1.44
Madurai	63.78	8.97	1.36	19.00	4.4	6.86
Visakhapatnam	52.95	5.02	0.0	36.55	4.42	1.06
Northern region						
Ludhiana and Jalandhar	15.50	15.66	0.00	67.87	0.52	0.45
Chandigarh	14.77	2.07	0.00	82.82	0.00	0.34
Jaipur	46.13	7.40	0.05	43.65	0.81	1.96
North-central						
Kanpur	59.82	9.61	0.00	30.58	0.00	0.00
Varanasi	53.48	31.22	0.00	15.25	0.05	0.00
Lucknow	9.59	19.37	0.01	69.97	0.72	0.34
Central						
Indore	33.98	28.33	0.00	36.31	0.68	0.69
Nagpur	22.63	34.40	0.00	38.48	3.82	0.66
Bhopal	57.23	29.71	0.00	12.83	0.22	0.00

Source: CMIE, CapEx database.

shows where the largest amount of investment has gone in nine of the leading cities of the country. However, as the financial details of all projects have not been disclosed to CMIE, the data are not complete. The proportion of total investment covered is indicated in the last row of the table.

What is clearly seen is that transport and communications have been a very important sector of investment accounting for over 50 per cent of the disclosed total in the four top cities. In Bengaluru, construction and infrastructure, which would include residential construction, has been more important. It has also been very important in Hyderabad, Ahmedabad, and Pune. Hospitals and healthcare services and hotels and recreation have seen considerable investment in all the nine cities. Investment in information technology (IT) as a proportion of the total investment in the city has been significant in Kolkata, Chennai, Bengaluru, Hyderabad, and Pune. The latter city has also had significant investment in auto and auto ancillaries.

Table 9 is reflective of investment patterns in the core areas of the larger cities. Investment patterns in the larger metropolitan region or the districts spilling over from the urban cores indicate not only

TABLE 9 Percentage Distribution of Major Investment by Industry Type in the Top Nine Cities, 1995–2010

Industry type	Mumbai	Delhi	Kolkata	Chennai	Bengaluru	Hydera-bad	Ahmeda-bad	Pune	Surat
Automobile and ancillaries	0.02	0.29	0	0.59	1.12	0.54	0.14	6.24	0.01
Transport and communications	64.07	71.66	62.24	51.97	0.94	41.01	40.44	35.19	13.39
Electronics	2.12	0.19	2.35	1.28	0.71	12.92	0.19	0.07	0
Construction and infrastructure	15.21	7.11	4.65	19.08	66.14	30.18	36.29	31.96	2.02
Information technology	0.41	0.98	6.69	4.58	8.12	3.22	0.91	3.42	0
Oil, gas, and power (not distribution)	0.03	6.45	7.86	6.62	4.26	0.09	7.72	10.12	48.59
Hospitals and health services	3.32	2.16	4.57	2.35	7.38	2.38	2.19	1.93	2.36
Hotels and recreation	11.22	8.46	9.27	5.28	3.98	6.92	3.69	5.54	1.03
Wholesale and retail	1.86	2.42	1.07	4.10	5.88	0.67	0.33	3.35	0.32
Qty disclosed to CMIE (Rs crore)	395932.1	229715.9	104729.4	213039.9	159799.15	166947.46	262402.89	188668.6	108521.8
% of total	79.11	66.47	57.71	73.55	46.24	62.53	78.32	69.57	37.47

Source: CMIE, CapEx database.

IT and ITES (information technology-enabled services) but also more manufacturing industries such as automobiles and their components, pharmaceuticals, and biotechnology, and garments and textiles. These areas have grown rapidly in the last two decades and demand for land in such locations continues to be very high for both industry as well as residential purposes.

The rapid growth of the peripheral areas of major cities has been both positive and negative. Their growth story post economic liberalization is not complete without mentioning the day-to-day difficulties of those living in extended city areas as well as the environmental impacts and ongoing conflicts over land.

Growth Pangs and Land Acquisition Conflicts

While the surrounding urban regions of most major Indian cities have seen growth in jobs and income, they suffer from a growing mismatch in the demand and supply of basic urban services, making them difficult to traverse and live in. In a recent *New York Times* article (Yardley 2011), this has been labelled as 'dysfunctionality' and has been contrasted with the cities' dynamic growth. Such dysfunctionality and economic dynamism going hand-in-hand is perhaps, best epitomized by the emerging city of Gurgaon, on the southern periphery of Delhi. As highlighted in the article, Gurgaon has twenty-six shopping malls, seven golf courses, shops and stores selling global luxury brands, and many IT firms and call centres but does not have a functioning sewerage system, proper water supply, decent roads, public transport, and garbage removal. Made into a municipal corporation in 2008, it has a long way to go to establish proper public services for its population of 1.5 million. While there are several private service providers for the higher income residential enclaves and commercial centres, the ordinary city dweller has to rough it out with uncertain or absent basic services. A lack of public services is especially harsh for the poor and the labouring class who cannot afford to buy basic services privately.

The edge of the city where the rural and urban meet has also been a zone of intense and ongoing conflicts over land with farmers resisting the moves of the government to take over land, stated to be 'in the public interest', to build urban infrastructure. From the well-known case of Singur, on the fringes of the Kolkata metropolitan region to the case of the Jamunanagar Highway in Noida, farmers have seen these attempts as unjust and unscrupulous. The government, on the other hand, eager for private investment, has often gone beyond strictly public interest and pandered to private developers and firms, acquiring more land than necessary. It has also acquired land cheaply, giving a pittance to land losers and then handing these parcels over to private developers who after development have reaped huge windfalls. Such glaring injustices in the government's land acquisition policy must be removed at the earliest to provide a smooth transition in the conversion of rural land uses to urban land uses, without which cities cannot grow.

3

Economic Activities of
Indian Cities

Currently, urban areas account for over 60 per cent of India's gross domestic product (GDP) and a significant share of this comes from the larger urban settlements of the country. In the last chapter, we looked at urban growth in the post-liberalization period and its effects such as the emergence of economically dynamic urban corridors and clusters of cities. We also looked at the economic activities characteristic of such areas. However, the emerging new economy of the dynamic urban regions does not constitute the entire gamut of urban economic activities and in this chapter, the focus is on the remainder of the urban economy, that is, both the so-called old economy and 'other' economic activities outside the formal sector that continue to be important. In fact, despite the attention that jobs in IT and ITES have been given both in the local media as well as internationally, they constitute a very small proportion of total urban jobs. The growth of the formal organized sector in India has slowed down since the 1980s and, unglamorous though it sounds, employment and livelihoods continue to be mostly in the informal sector.

The term 'informal sector' as used in this chapter refers to that section of the workforce that is not covered by protective legislation and is characterized by low incomes and lack of job security. Such workers include not only wage earners employed in small-scale enterprises but also subcontracted labourers in large factories and the vast numbers that undertake different types of home-based work for larger units or middlemen. The informal sector also comprises small units or enterprises run by families and/or hired labour, producing goods or selling goods and services. It includes a wide range of low-level service workers who may have more than one employer or customer. Thus, wage work with varying degrees of stability/permanence and self-employment with varying levels of earnings constitute the two main forms of work in the informal sector.

What Kind of Economic Activities Dominate Indian Cities?

We begin with this simple question and to answer it we need to look at the distribution of broad economic activities in India's urban areas. This is shown in Table 10 for three time periods, 1987–8, 1993–4, and 1999–2000 thus giving us a view of conditions prior to economic liberalization and post liberalization. Urban areas have been classified into small towns, medium towns, and large towns on the basis of population size with small towns having less than 50,000 people, medium towns having between 50,000 and 1 million, and large towns having over 1 million people.

What is interesting to note from Table 10 is the fact that despite the gradual deindustrialization of the city core that began in the early 1980s, manufacturing remains an important activity with a relatively constant share through the twelve-year period, though across the different size classes of towns, a slight decline is seen. Prior to liberalization in 1987–8, manufacturing was the principal industry of 23 per cent of urban households and in 1999–2000 of 22 per cent urban households. In the million plus cities, where the contribution of manufacturing has been larger as compared to smaller towns, the decline has been sharper. On the other hand, agriculture and its related activities continue to be important in small towns where 17 per cent of households were earning from agriculture in 1999–2000. For urban areas of all sizes, there has been a significant increase in wholesale and retail trade, restaurants, and hotels. In fact, this increase has primarily occurred after 1993–4. Urban households in transport, storage, and communication activities have also increased from 9 per cent in 1987–8 to 11 per cent in 1999–2000. Finally, there has been a noticeable decline in community, social, and personal services in all size classes of towns.

Table 10 provides only a very broad distribution of urban households by major types of economic activity and each of the nine categories is an aggregation of numerous subcategories of occupations. Thus for instance, under Item 9, community, social, and personal services, the aggregate declining trend does not reveal the fact that certain types of personal services such as that of maids, cooks, beauticians are in fact increasing in Indian cities. Also, it indicates very little about the quality of work and for this we need to consider the structure of the urban labour market.

TABLE 10 Industrial Distribution: Urban Households

Year and towns by size	0 Agriculture, hunting, and forestry	1 Mining and quarry-ing	2 and 3 Manu-facturing	4 Electricity, gas, and water	5 Construc-tion	6 Trade and hotels	7 Transport, storage, and communi-cations	8 Finance and real estate	9 Comm-unity services
1987–8									
Small	16.7	2.4	17.5	1.6	5.5	18.2	7.8	3.0	27.4
Medium	4.9	1.0	24.7	1.4	5.1	19.9	10.1	4.2	28.7
Large	1.3	0.1	28.0	1.4	5.1	21.1	10.6	6.6	25.7
All	8.4	1.3	22.8	1.4	5.2	19.5	9.4	4.2	27.7
1993–4									
Small	22.5	2.7	17.7	1.7	5.5	18.1	8.6	2.3	20.8
Medium	10.2	1.2	21.6	1.2	6.2	20.3	10.7	3.6	24.9
Large	5.2	0.2	25.6	1.4	6.5	19.0	10.4	6.2	25.2
All	13.0	1.5	21.3	1.4	6.1	19.4	10.0	3.7	23.7
1999–2000									
Small	16.8	2.2	16.7	1.5	9.0	23.5	9.1	2.9	18.4
Medium	5.4	1.0	22.6	1.2	8.7	25.2	11.4	4.0	20.6
Large	1.5	0.1	26.2	0.6	7.6	25.1	12.6	6.0	20.2
All	7.7	1.1	21.8	1.1	8.5	24.7	11.0	4.2	19.8

Source: NSS unit-level data for various years as cited from Himangshu (2007:Table 11).

Structure of the Urban Labour Market

The National Sample Survey Organization (NSSO) in its 61st Round has provided information on important aspects of the urban labour market such as the contribution of the formal and the informal sector and the broad kinds of work prevalent in 2004–5.

Of the total of around 84 million employed in urban areas in 2004–5, the NSS found that 75 per cent were employed in the informal sector and 25 per cent in the formal sector. Work has been categorized by the NSS into three broad types as self-employment, regular work, and casual work. In terms of quality of job and pay, casual work is the least preferred and is associated with poverty. Taking into consideration both male and female workers, self-employment accounted for 44 per cent of the workforce, regular wage work for 42 per cent, and casual work for around 14 per cent. Interesting is the fact that the 42 per cent in regular wage work was almost equally divided between the formal sector and the informal sector. The formal sector accounted for around 22 per cent while the informal sector accounted for 20 per cent. Thus nearly half of the regular wage work in the labour force is coming from the informal sector. While about 80 per cent of the workforce comprised male workers, self-employed males in the informal sector constituted about 34 per cent of the work force. For females too, the pattern is the same with the bulk of those employed working in the informal sector.

Quite clearly, despite two decades of economic liberalization and growth of the new economy, the informal sector is still the predominant sector of employment in Indian cities, both for men and women. This is a very important feature of Indian cities and is generally lost sight of in the popular press which gives much greater coverage to the new economy. It is interesting also to note the urban activities where the informal sector is concentrated and those activities that are predominantly formal in a typical Indian city. The NSS provides this information as well and it is shown in Table 11.

Male workers in the informal sector are concentrated in trade and manufacturing which together accounted for 60 per cent of the jobs in that sector. If construction and transport are added the total comes to 82 per cent. For females in the informal sector, it is trade, manufacturing, and working in private households

TABLE 11 Informal Sector and Formal Sector Presence in Different Kinds of Urban Work, 2004–5 (per cent)

Industrial classification of urban work	Distribution of IS male workers	Distribution of FS male workers	Share of informal segment	Distribution of IS female workers	Distribution of FS female workers	Share of informal segment
Wholesale and retail trade	34	4	97	14	2	97
Manufacturing	26	22	79	41	13	91
Construction	11	5	88	5	2	90
Transport, storage, and communications	11	12	75	1	4	49
Hotels and restaurants	5	1	95	4	0	97
Real estate, renting, and business activities	4	4	78	2	3	64
Other community, social, and personal services	4	2	82	5	2	90
Education	2	10	34	8	36	42
Financial intermediation	1	7	29	0	7	18
Health and social work	1	3	55	2	11	42
Private households with employed persons	1	0	99	17	1	98
Mining and quarrying	0	3	25	0	1	43
Electricity, gas, and water supply	0	3	9	0	1	2
Public administration and defence	0	25	1	0	17	1
	100	100		100	100	

Source: NSSO 61st Round, as cited from Mukhopadhyay (2011).

Note: IS = informal sector; FS = formal sector.

which together accounted for 73 per cent of informal sector jobs. Overall, the share of the informal sector in these kinds of work is very high. Male employment in the formal sector is high in manufacturing and transport, and also in education, financial intermediation, and public administration. Females in the formal sector are concentrated in manufacturing, education, health and social work, and public administration. Thus other than manufacturing, the formal and informal segments of the labour market seem to be catering to different aspects of the urban economy: the formal segment on services such as finance, education, and governance and the informal segment on trade, transport, and construction. The two segments clearly complement each other in the urban economy of Indian cities. It is these complementarities that are the basis of the economy of Indian cities, providing them with great absorptive capacity and flexibility in the organization of work and delivery of services.

Turning to details of occupations and which ones are flourishing in Indian cities post-liberalization, NSS data reveal that while the service sector has grown, growth of jobs in services has occurred in both the formal and informal sectors. The demand for teachers, maids, cooks, chauffeurs, healthcare workers, tailors and dressmakers, beauticians and hairdressers has gone up with rising incomes. Some of these jobs blur the line between formal and informal as when a formal establishment, for instance, a large restaurant has hired workers without a contract or social security. On the other hand, a so-called informal sector job, for instance, that of a family chauffeur or maid, could provide steady employment for years and include wage increments and holidays. Since finding domestic help is not easy, many personal services are becoming more regularized. Similarly, job regularization is also starting to occur in small-scale manufacturing, trade, commerce, and finance where high worker turnover hits the enterprise very hard making it difficult to compete, particularly if such units have direct or indirect global linkages. The gradual formalization of the informal sector is particularly well seen in the domestic service sector.

Service Sector Growth and Domestic Services

In the last two decades, as India's service sector has been growing at unprecedented rates, many service sector jobs have been created and these are mostly in the cities. One occupation that has seen huge growth is that of domestic service. This occupation has a long history of association with migration into urban areas but in the last two decades, it has been 'reinvented' in new and unique forms.

Domestic service involves working in private homes in tasks such as housecleaning, laundry, cooking, washing dishes, care of children and the aged, shopping for groceries, fetching and dropping children from/to school, as well as other activities necessary for the smooth functioning of the household. While men have been hired for domestic work, the occupation is overwhelmingly dominated by women who are seen as being more suitable as these are tasks they perform in their own households. From the point of view of illiterate women, other than cooking, these tasks require little training and can be easily performed after a few directions from the employer.

Growth in domestic service and its increasingly gendered profile is seen from macro data provided by the NSSO. In five years, between 1999–2000 and 2004–5, the number of domestic workers increased by 2.25 million. This includes both the so-called 'live-in' workers and the 'live-out' workers. Live-in workers reside with the employers' household, going back to their own homes once or twice a year, during brief vacations. Live-out workers are employed in several households but stay in their own residences. In 2004–5, there were 4.75 million workers employed in private households of which 3.05 million were women (64 per cent) and they were working in urban areas. The percentage of domestic workers in total female employment in the service sector also increased from around 12 per cent in 1999–2000 to 27 per cent in 2004–5.

While the supply of domestic workers can be explained by a surplus of unskilled workers in the poor regions of the country, agrarian crisis, loss of jobs of male family members or their chronic unemployment, and desertion/abandonment by male members and the consequent need for females to support the family, it is the demand side that is more interesting in the sense that it throws light on demographic and lifestyle changes occurring in the cities and explains the puzzle of why there is an increasing need for domestic services by the urban middle class in spite of more white goods and labour-saving household gadgets. First, there has been an increase in the absolute numbers of middle-class women entering the labour market in the cities. The number and proportion of adolescent girls who are in school or college has also been increasing. Absence of female members during the working day necessitates the hiring of domestic workers. Second, the growth in nuclear families in urban areas means that older generation females are no longer present in the household to help and outside assistance is needed. Third, there is the affordability of domestic services. Apart from cooking, other kinds of domestic work are regarded as unskilled and wages are low. So, in middle-class households, washing machines and maids coexist, with the maid washing clothes that are not suitable for the machine. Similarly, in the kitchen, labour-saving gadgets like mixers can coexist with the traditional stone grinder for hand-grinding special spices.

A key aspect of domestic service is its relationship to migration. Most domestic workers are migrants, either first-generation or second-generation. The growth in domestic workers in the last two decades has largely been of the 'live-outs' who perform specific tasks within different households but have their own residences.

A high proportion of live-outs are from slums and squatter settlements within walking distance of their workplaces. In Delhi, there has been a regular flow of live-outs from local squatter settlements comprising migrants who have come to the capital from rural pockets in UP, Bihar, and West Bengal. Live-ins, on the other hand, are younger, unmarried, with some education and originate predominantly from the tribal regions of Jharkhand, Chhattisgarh, Orissa, Assam, and West Bengal. They are mostly Christian, and they head for cities such as Delhi, Mumbai, and Bengaluru. Live-in work is gradually becoming more formalized with the emergence of placement agencies.

In fact, these placement agencies are 'reinventing' and institutionalizing an old form of informal labour supply to urban areas. Today, most metropolitan cities in India have placement agencies for domestic service, managed by private entrepreneurs as well as by voluntary associations. Their agents visit villages to recruit women for work in the cities. To protect them from exploitation, in some of the tribal regions, the church has become an important agency in facilitating the migration of domestic workers to the cities.

Complementarities of the Formal and Informal Sectors

As mentioned earlier, there are many complementarities between the formal and the informal sector in Indian cities. It is these complementarities that have enabled Indian cities to reach out to all economic categories of people. An area of concern is that the complementarities could be slowly unravelling with the continued liberalization of the economy, and larger corporate players gradually entering activities which have so far been small-scale or informal. One such area is retail trade in food and groceries where foreign investment has not yet been permitted but domestic investment in large-format markets and hypermarkets has been allowed as in the case of the Reliance outlets, Big Bazaar, and Spencer's. These, however, fulfil a middle-class need and have been doing well in most cities. A key to the successful transition of India's cities would be allowing both formal and informal retail trade to coexist rather than the formal sector wiping out the informal as has been feared by small shopkeepers and roadside vendors. These fears have been heightened with the UPA (United Progressive Alliance) government's announcement in December 2011 of permitting

51 per cent foreign investment in multi-brand retail. What follows is the case of one large-scale retail project that has through a long and protracted process of negotiation resulted in the accommodation of small, licensed traders and vendors as well as the informal sector.

Lake Market is one of Kolkata Municipal Corporation's (KMC) twenty-three markets. Most of the KMC markets occupy prime land and are sprawling, one-storey structures, generally in a poor condition. By the 1980s, several were already very dilapidated and cramped for space and there was growing realization that direct and immediate attention was needed to save these markets in the physical sense. It was also realized that given the locations of most of the markets in densely populated older neighbourhoods where land is scarce, the new building projects must be vertical. Facing a shortage of funds, the KMC began to give serious thought to inviting private developers to upgrade the markets. In May 1986, bids from private developers were sought through open tender in the newspapers for three KMC markets including Lake Market which is located at the intersection of two busy roads, Rashbehari Avenue and Lake Road, in the southern part of the city, in Ward 87.

This Ward is located in south Kolkata which historically is newer than the north and central portions of
the city. However, as the city and its suburbs have continued to expand both southwards and east, these areas
are no longer new. In fact, Ward 87 like a number of
older wards in the north and central parts of the city
has started losing population. Its growth rate of population during 1991–2001 was -28 per cent as its total
population had fallen from 18,534 in 1991 to 13,324
in 2001. Although KMC's objective in market upgra-
dation was driven by the poor condition of the existing
market and the possibility of earning more revenues
through creating more space by vertical expansion,
the project had implications beyond these. Given
the increasing popularity of large-format retail shopping located in malls coming up in the newer parts
of the city where space has not been a constraint, the
older portions of the city have been losing custom-
ers and economic dynamism. New market projects in
older neighbourhoods have the potential of raising the
attractiveness of such localities.

Following from the bidding process launched by
KMC in 1986, Arun Plastics (now renamed Venkatesh
Foundation) was chosen by the KMC Technical

Committee and an agreement was signed on the 29 June 1987 to redevelop the old Lake Market, 4,483 sq. m in area. In 1988, the developer began building temporary sheds for the stall owners of the market but local trouble stopped all work. The trouble, spearheaded by a local opposition leader, was over the issue of what the stall owners would do in the interim period when the market was being built and from where they would operate during this time. There was also the issue of whether they would all be reinstated inside the new market or would the new space be auctioned to outside traders willing to pay higher taxes after the betterment. On the government's side, the first clause of the agreement with the developer had stated that there would be complete rehabilitation of all existing stall owners in the new market. But no amount of convincing on the part of government and its emissaries could reduce this mistrust and work stoppage continued. In 1989, with losses mounting and amid fears of bid-cancellation for non-work, Arun Plastics went to court. The court placed a stay-order on all construction while it considered the case. In 1996, the Kolkata High Court gave its verdict and it was in favour of Arun Plastics. It was to continue as the developer and no fresh bids were required. However, almost nine years had passed since the agreement had first been signed.

In these nine years, there was further deterioration of the physical structure of the old market and there was even an incident of a huge piece of the ceiling falling off and almost killing some traders. This situation led to a rethinking by many vendors and the realization that perhaps there was something positive in the redevelopment plans of the government. In the meantime, there were some local-level political changes. An important change was the winning of the Ward 87 council seat by Subrata Mukherjee of the Trinamul Congress and his being elected Mayor of the Kolkata Municipal Corporation in 2000. As a councillor representing Ward 87 and mayor of the city, he saw the redevelopment as an opportunity and pushed the stalled project through. Work began again and in 2002, the old one-storey market was demolished. Vendors were given a rehabilitation package for the transition period by the developer. This was of two kinds: some of the vendors were accommodated along the pavements surrounding the market. They were allowed to set up their stalls there. But as such space was limited there were vendors who were compensated with money, their average monthly earnings for two years given as a lump sum. Some used the money to open new stalls elsewhere while others just took a break and awaited the completion of the new market.

Features of the Project

The redevelopment of Lake Market was undertaken as a BOT (build, operate, transfer) project with the builder having a sixty-year lease of the property. Since 2002, progress has been satisfactory and the new structure has now come up on the old plot with the ground floor completely done by 2007. All the old vendors were reinstated in their various stalls on the ground floor and they resumed their activities. However, the upper floors still needed completion and April 2009 was the government's opening date for the new market but that was deferred till after the state assembly elections of May 2011. The new market is a seven-storey structure (G + 6) with the old market occupying the entire ground floor which continues to be managed by the KMC. In addition, another 1,000 sq. m on the fourth floor, will be given to KMC for its use as a Citizens'

Centre. The additional space being created in the new building will be leased to large retail firms such as Big Bazaar and Globus. It will also contain a food court and multiplex theatre. Ward 87 does not have any large cinema and the multiplex theatre was planned by the developer after taking feedback from long-term local residents. Thus the new businesses have the potential to draw the local population as well as that from other parts of the city back to Lake Market for shopping and recreational needs.

Impact of the New Market on the Old Market Vendors

We now turn to the all-important issue of resettlement of the vendors in the old market. The ground floor of the new structure is where all the vendors of the old market have been resettled. They include stall holders, slab holders, and day vendors of the old market, numbering a total of 350. The spaces that they occupy are identical in size to their spaces in the old market. Along with the stall holders there are their hired helpers such as the fish cleaners and cutters, and the head loaders who depend on the market for a living. They too have returned and resumed their old jobs.

The ambience of the ground floor is similar to the old market with the vendors having decorated their stalls in their own way. The arrangement broadly follows the structure of the old market with meat, fish, and poultry shops in a separate unit and the rest of the ground floor roughly separated into sections such as vegetables and fruits, dry groceries, household items, and so on. The market continues to have a traditional feel and ambience and thus retains its diversity.

FIGURE 3   Resettled vendors on the ground floor of the new market

Source: Photograph taken by author, 2009.

The fear that redevelopment leads to homogenization and loss of unique local cultural traits and that the built environment becomes 'placeless' has been proved wrong in this case. Moreover, while retaining its local flavour, the market's upkeep and maintenance is much better, for instance, the stalls are well-lit and the vendors have access to basic facilities that they had previously lacked, for example, a toilet, drinking water, and a changing room.

An important question is whether the old market, rehabilitated on the ground floor of the new structure, will be able to survive in the medium to long run with the new, smart shops above it. It is difficult to give any answer with certainty but according to an all-India study conducted by the Indian Council for Research on International Economic Relations in 2008, the impact of organized retail on unorganized retail is more complex than a simple yes or no to the above question. The main findings of the study are as follows: first, a decline in the volume of business and profit in the initial years but the adverse impact weakens over time; second, there is no evidence of a decline in the overall employment in unorganized retail; and third, with retail business in India expected to grow at 13 per cent per

FIGURE 4   Ambience of the old market has remained intact
Source: Photograph taken by author, 2009.

annum till 2011–12, unorganized and organized retail can coexist. But work done by other researchers has not been so optimistic. In the case of Lake Market, Big Bazaar, the supermarket will apparently not be selling products that compete with the old market, namely, fruits, vegetables, meat, fish, and other groceries. This was communicated to me by several stall holders on a visit to the market in December 2010. Whether this policy will actually be implemented once the store is opened, remains to be seen.

A second issue is the official opening of the new market complex itself, which was delayed till after the state assembly elections of May 2011, although the structure was completed many months back. But, today, even after one year of Mamata Banerjee coming to power, the new market remains unused except for the ground floor which houses the old market. As in the older markets of the city, the new market has been surrounded by informal stalls which have attached themselves to its walls, on all sides. The formal and informal sector have been thus coexisting but as some

FIGURE 5 The informal sector has attached itself to the sides of the mall

Source: Photograph taken by author, 2010.

of the informal units are blocking the entrance and exit points to the new market, it is likely that they will be removed. Interestingly, the small stall owners reinstated from the old market are in favour of the eviction of the vendors and hawkers outside the market seeing them as unlicensed competitors.

★ ★ ★

This detailed case-study of the kind of economic conflict happening between the formal and informal segments within Indian cities shows the multilayered nature of the issues involved. Within the informal sector are gradations of informality and job insecurity and the sector should not be viewed as a monolith. Likewise, the so-called formal sector too has gradations of formality and job security and all workers within it are not necessarily well-off with secure incomes. Thus while the binaries, formal and informal, help us to easily visualize how work in Indian cities is organized, they have limitations which extend particularly to issues of economic class and social identity. The next chapter turns to the issue of economic class as reflected in the changing cityscape.

4

The Changing Cityscape

This chapter turns to the visual aspects of the Indian city or why Indian cities look the way they do. Lack of identifiable form and sharp contrasts in wealth and poverty have contributed to the production of a complex and plural landscape that defies easy categorization. Mixed land uses combining residential with commercial and other economic uses, a hallmark of pre-colonial urbanism, have persisted through colonialism into the post-independence years and remain a distinctive feature of Indian cities. Even highly planned residential suburbs, with time, begin to display some non-residential uses. The characteristic appearance of Indian cities has also been the product of a pluralistic cultural history, changing economic functions, and the state's material presence in the local area via buildings housing its activities and institutions. It has also been affected by the state's policies on land and housing. In this chapter too, a formal/informal segmentation of the city can be helpful to understand the complexity and change, enabling us to visualize the landscape in terms of a 'static city' comprising the built environment made of more permanent materials such as concrete, steel and brick, and a 'kinetic city' which is temporary in nature, built of plastic, sheets, scrap metal, and other leftovers. The kinetic city is a city in motion, constantly having to adapt and change and is captured in activities such as processions, weddings, festivals, street vending and in informal land uses such as the *kutcha* housing associated with slums and squatter settlements.

These two kinds of cities have always coexisted in the same physical space as part of an indigenous organic urbanism but during colonial times, began to be seen as two distinct entities. The idea of formal as different and legitimate compared to the informal became encoded in colonial bureaucratic lexicon and practices to enable ordering and management of India's chaotic urban areas. During the post-independence nationalist phase of urbanization the informal sector's presence continued to be tolerated as offering alternative spaces for the poor to live and work in the city. Also, though less acknowledged, slums and squatter settlements acted as sources of cheap labour for the formal economy and as sites of small factories and workshops that produced cheap goods. After 1991 and the rapid growth experienced in many of the larger cities, population densities have increased and so has the demand for urban land. The coexistence of the formal and the informal sectors is now being challenged in many ways, setting up an ongoing scenario of intense interaction as well as conflict.

Two processes stand out post-1991: (i) gentrification or the gradual takeover of land for use by the upper middle and middle classes and (ii) informalization, that is, a process of incremental expansion of the informal economy responding to the needs of both the poor and the middle class. Gentrification, a process familiar to cities in advanced countries, is generally associated with a displacement of poor communities by rich outsiders. When wealthier people move into a neighbourhood, there is an increase in rents and property values and changes in the neighbourhood's character and culture. Informalization, on the other hand, is unique to cities in poorer countries. It is the process by which informal economic activities and informal housing gain access to existing spaces in the city and its fringes. We will look at the effect of both these processes as we turn to the broad influences shaping the landscape of Indian cities.

Cultural Diversity

The influence of cultural pluralism on the cityscape can be seen both through the lens of the static city as well as the kinetic city. In contemporary cities, the richness and diversity of India's cultural past is not necessarily confined to a historic precinct or quarter where it is reflected in buildings of similar age, style and arrangement as for instance in the old walled parts of Ahmedabad. It could well encompass several other wards or zones of the city. It can be seen, for instance, in the juxtaposition of buildings belonging to different eras as in Bengaluru's administrative core where the skyline reflects the presence of a pre-colonial, colonial, and post-colonial past. It is also seen in many of Mumbai's older wards in the various vertical heights and housing styles. In fact a total of twenty-one housing typologies have been identified in south and central Mumbai which together reflect its historical past from its inception as a fishing village in the 1600s, to its position as a colonial port, its transformation into an industrial city post-independence, and its current existence. The fishing community built its houses in a distinct way, as did the trader-merchants, the colonial masters and the early post-independent state. These are all reflected in the diverse skyline of the built environment of Mumbai.

The skyline of Indian cities is also etched by the steeples of churches and the domes of mosques, gurdwaras and temples. The largest of these form distinct landmarks in the city adding to its heritage and attractiveness. While large temples are surrounded by a mini-economy of small shops and stalls selling flowers, incense, and all the paraphernalia needed for a puja, the neighbourhoods of large mosques are not just commercial but can also be a preferred residential location of the local Muslim community. Thus there could be a distinct Muslim quarter or neighbourhood around the main mosque of the city.

At the street level, cultural pluralism in Indian cities is seen in the many kinds of religious buildings often coexisting within a short distance of each other.

Smaller temples, mosques, and churches can all occur along one street with their associated festivities, such as roadside fairs during major festivals, and processions. Less commonly, it can also occur around a shared public space such as a square, as in the hill town of Nainital.

FIGURE 6   Nainital—Main square
Source: Photograph taken by author, 2009.

Like the large and small religious buildings which are gathering places for people of different religions and are part of the built environment, so are the cemeteries and crematoria. The cemeteries built during colonial times are a rich repository of the city's history and often occupy central parts of the city as in the case of Kolkata's South Park Street Cemetery built in 1767.

Along with the permanent and fixed structures of the built environment that reflect the city's culture, there are a host of activities that extend public spaces in the city to allow for the people's enjoyment of religious festivals such as Diwali, Navratri, Dussera, Durga Puja, Muharram, Ganesh Chaturthi, and Chhat Puja. In the case of Ganesh Puja and Durga Puja, the leading festivals of Mumbai and Kolkata, respectively, city neighbourhoods are transformed into elaborate puja venues with lights and decoration. New public spaces are created to house the idols for a week to ten days, often usurping main roads and pavements. The Durga Puja pandals of Kolkata reflect different themes and even political issues, at once turning the venues into sites of multiple enjoyments, religious and secular. The popularity of these festivals, held largely in public spaces, has only grown over the years such that they have become a powerful expression of the popular culture of Indian cities.

Just as the puja pandals with their lights, decorations, queuing crowds, and loudspeaker music temporarily alter the landscape of the city, so do the activities of another popular pastime, cricket watching and playing. Like the celebrations for different festivals, this spills over onto the street and is indulged in by both the middle class and the urban poor. At the height of cricket fever, as during the semi-final and final of the World Cup of 2011, middle class residential areas had giant screens for collective viewing while in slums and squatter settlements, people crowded together over a television set. When India won, it was 10 o'clock at night, a time when public transport is minimal. The rich and upper middle class rushed to the streets in their cars and the middle class and the poor by foot to gather at points and collectively scream and shout and celebrate the victory.

Thus the kinetic city is not necessarily the city of the poor as both the rich and the poor can occupy public space temporarily to extend the boundaries of their habitable area in order to fulfil certain needs.

From Manufacturing to Services

Changes in economic functions within a city can have a major effect on the way a city looks. The gradual shift from manufacturing to service and information-based activities experienced globally since the late 1960s and by India from the 1980s, has left its mark on the cities in profound ways. With textile mills and factories closing down, the sale of their land in the open market has given private developers an opportunity to develop projects on a scale previously only allowed to the government. Such large-scale projects of urban redevelopment are happening in those cities that had a significant industrial base centred on textiles and machinery. The most famous of these are Mumbai's mill lands which together cover over 608 acres. Such large pieces of land, now available as the manufacturing industry leaves these locations, are also to be found in Kolkata, for instance, 262 acres in the case of the Bata factory, 61 acres in the case of the Siemen's plant, and 31 acres in the case of Usha Fans. The latter site has been converted into 'South City', an integrated retail and high-income residential complex, by a consortium of the city's top seven private developers. It contains the city's tallest residential complex and one of its biggest shopping malls.

Started in 2003, the transformation of the 31 acres has been from a derelict factory site overgrown with weeds to a posh shopping mall with a seven-storey

FIGURE 7   South City residential complex, Kolkata
Source: Photograph taken by author, 2011.

parking space for 1,500 cars, an international school
with a lush green playfield, four thirty-five-storey residential towers encircling a green area the size of Eden
Garden, the city's famous cricket stadium, and a luxurious club house with its own residential tower under
construction. Land and property values have already
risen dramatically with the cost per square foot of flats
more than doubling in six to seven years. The influx of
the well-to-do has had a cascading effect on the cost of
services provided by the informal sector, for instance,
maids, drivers, and laundry services.

While some of the most spectacular transformations have occurred in the old mill district of Girangaon in central Mumbai and on vacated factory land in Delhi, Ahmedabad, and Kolkata, it is increasingly occurring in other cities as well. Even smaller metropolitan cities such as Pune are experiencing this.

These large urban redevelopment projects mark a shift in building style and ethos which Brugmann has aptly called 'city-modelling'. Here a standardized product conceived and executed by developers takes the form of 'big-box structures' such as shopping malls, high-rise residential towers, and office spaces. Their massive scale makes them stand out in the Indian urban milieu, and their names and the high-profile advertisements that have gone to promote their sale, stress upon their cosmopolitan/global ambience and standards, or the quality of not being like the rest of the city or even the country. In South City's residential complex, the four thirty-five-storey towers have been named Oak, Maple, Pine, and Cedar to give the feel of being abroad, a tactic widely used in high-end real estate projects across the country.

Such projects have also created gated communities with high security and restricted entry for both humans and animals. An unexpected problem faced in the hurly-burly of urban India is the entry of stray dogs into the 'pristine' compounds of such communities. With its upper-income residents, many of whom own foreign pets, the *desi* dogs are to be feared and removed as they may harm their costly pets. Restriction can also happen in the case of religion, with residential complexes having only Hindu temples as places of religious worship.

In these senses, in the gated communities, there is a lack of tolerance for plurality and its accompanying untidiness that marks the rest of the Indian city. They represent a new and exclusive environment that has been purposely created to be orderly, clean, and with sharp boundaries. They reflect the increasingly disengaged nature of the rich and upper classes in urban India who want to be left alone to enjoy their lives and not be disturbed by the heterogeneous clamour of the city.

Apart from the large-scale urban redevelopment projects, gentrification is also to be seen in smaller processes of change. In fact, small-scale and often, building by building redevelopment has always been occurring in urban India but it has picked up speed in the last two decades. An old property is bought by a private developer who then develops it to accommodate several flats/apartments for residential uses or to supply office space. The impact of such transformation can be seen in the core areas of several cities, notably Mumbai where single-family detached bungalows in south Mumbai are being converted to multi-storey apartments. Likewise in Delhi where old suburbs such as the Rajendra Nagars that developed after Partition in 1947 with one-storey and two-storey residential structures are now almost all four to five storeys high.

State's Shrinking Physical Presence

In the early post-independence decades, when the state was in control of the commanding heights of the economy and much else besides, the physical space of Indian cities was marked by its buildings, created to house new institutions and organizations as well as its staff and workers. In fact, the state was and continues to be the single largest owner of land in any city if ownership by the different levels of government, namely, the central, state, and local government is taken together. This is partly a legacy of the past for during colonial times, the defeat of different rulers was followed by the annexation of their territories by the East India Company and after 1857, by the British Raj. The colonial state also confiscated private lands as punishment and there are records for the city of Delhi where the state confiscated the lands of all noblemen suspected of being involved in the revolt of 1857. The postcolonial state inherited all these lands as well as those private lands that were left without claimants or heirs when the British left India in 1947. In addition, it has also continued the practice of land confiscation or 'vesting', a process by which it can expropriate private land. This can be done in the 'public interest' to create necessary infrastructure in the built-up areas of the city but is more common on the fringes of the city. In the case of Kolkata's fringes, vesting has occurred via the confiscation of agricultural land in excess of the agricultural land ceilings, the confiscation of non-agricultural land in excess of urban land ceilings and the acquisition of land in the public interest by public agencies.

With the ownership of so much urban land, the state's policies and uses of urban land can have significant effects. In fact, from the time of independence up till the end of the 1980s, the state was a significant player in determining the built environment of the 'static city' or the city of fixed and permanent structures. Given its multifarious needs in the aftermath of Partition and independence, the state was the biggest client and most well-known buildings were built with state patronage. Second, many of these buildings were executed by public agencies such as the central and state public works departments, urban development authorities, and state housing boards. Thus during the nationalist period, 1947 till 1991, the most prominent buildings were *sarkari* or governmental and they dominated the administrative core of the city. While some executive and judicial functions continued in buildings inherited from colonial times, new buildings were created to house the new and more development-oriented functions of the postcolonial state. Some of these were to leave a major impression on the city as in the case of New Delhi, where buildings such as Vayu Bhavan, Krishi Bhavan, Udyog Bhavan, Rail Bhavan, Vigyan Bhavan, and the Supreme Court, all built in the 1950s by the Central Public Works Department, continue to be important landmarks.

Apart from public buildings that housed various offices and institutions of government, the state was an important contributor to residential housing in the city in the form of housing quarters for government employees and housing colonies built for refugees and the middle class. These are still visible in any Indian city, large or small, and are characterized by a distinctive style, the 'PWD style', of two to three-storey buildings with four to six flats of generally two rooms, a kitchen, bathroom, latrine, and a small balcony/veranda. But increasingly, such housing is being redeveloped into units with higher vertical height and more overcrowding as the open shared spaces are needed for parking cars, sometimes with more than one car per family.

Overall, the state's physical presence in the city, in its various forms, still remains but its public buildings, once new and striking as harbingers of the democratic modernism of post-independent India, are now dwarfed by the massive post-modern structures of glitzy shopping malls, corporate towers and upscale residential complexes dominating the skyline in different parts of the city. Likewise, the residential accommodation built by the state constitutes but a very small proportion of the total urban housing, only around 16 per cent.

Thus over 80 per cent of urban housing is private and provided via two parallel systems, the formal and the informal. The formal private sector is made up of small and large developers, housing cooperatives as well as owners of plots hiring local architects and *mistri*s to build their homes. The informal sector is the much larger component and covers illegal processes of land occupancy such as squatting or land invasion as well as the development of unauthorized colonies by middle and lower income groups. In older cities, there is a third component to private housing, and it is represented by legally built structures in the older parts of the city which are generally characterized by dilapidated and overcrowded conditions, low levels of basic services and lower-income residents. This is called organic housing since it can predate the modern city, as for example, the Koli or fishing community's settlement in Mumbai or urban villages such as Haus Khas in New Delhi that pre-existed the urban development around them.

Residential houses in Indian cities are thus a product of multiple agencies, formal, informal, and organic, and they have left their distinctive mark on the city and contributed to the heterogeneity and diversity of the built environment. While organic and informal buildings tend to be low-rises, the buildings of the formal private sector are increasingly high-rises to support the high cost of land, allow for open green spaces, and guarantee a sky-view of the city and the feeling of being far away and above the din and dirt.

State's Policies

The dominance of the private sector in house-building activities today is not something that has just happened post economic liberalization. It is mistakenly thought by some that the present situation, where around 84 per cent of housing stock in Indian cities is created by the private sector, is an outcome of a conscious policy followed by the state, over the last two decades, to retreat from building activities and to give more visibility to the private sector in real estate, housing, and infrastructure building. In reality, this has a much longer history and goes back to the early days of nationalist planning. At that time, and continuing into subsequent decades, despite its importance, housing received very low priority in India's public policy and investment programmes, and while some piecemeal programmes did exist, much of the supply of housing was left to the market. Unfortunately, the market was not able to keep up with the demand for housing and in particular, housing for the poor. Squatter settlements and unauthorized colonies of the informal housing market are the visible manifestations of the failure of both the state and the market to keep pace with the growing demand.

The poor, out-priced in the formal housing market and without the safety net provided by state-subsidized housing, increasingly resorted to occupying whatever land they could find in the city and this included footpaths, sides of roads, unused open areas, and environmentally undesirable areas such as swamps and sides of rivers and canals.

In the densely populated mega-cities such as Kolkata and Mumbai, formal and informal housing exist side by side and merge into each other as in the following evocative description of Mumbai's housing by Arjun Appadurai in 2007:

> ... there is a vast range of insecure housing, from a six-foot stretch of sleeping space to a poorly defined tenancy situation shared by three families 'renting' one room. Pavements shade into *jopad-patti*s (complexes of shacks with few amenities), which shade into semi-permanent illegal structures. Another continuum links these structures to *chawl*s (tenement housing originally

built for mill workers in Central Bombay) and to other forms of substandard housing. Above this tier are the owned or rented flats of the large middle class and finally the fancy flats and (in a tiny number of cases) houses owned by the rich and the super rich. These kinds of housing are not neatly segregated by neighborhood, for one simple reason: the insecurely housed poor are everywhere and are only partly concentrated in *basti*s (slums), jopad-pattis, and chawls. Almost every one of these kinds of housing for the poor, including roofs, parapets, compound walls, and overhangs, is subject to socially negotiated arrangements. Very often, control over these insecure spaces is in the hands of semi-organized crime, where rent and extortion shade into one another.

Even in the apartment buildings of the rich and upper middle class … there is a constant pressure from the house poor. The poor set up house anywhere they can light a fire and stretch out a thin sheet to sleep on. As domestic servants, they often have small rooms in the large apartment buildings of the rich, and these servants (for whom such housing is a huge privilege) often bring friends and dependents, who spill out into the stairwells, the enclosed compounds, and the foyers. The official tenants, owners, and landlords wage a constant war against this colonization from below, but it is frequently lost because—as in all societies based on financial apartheid—one wants the poor near at hand as servants but far away as humans.

At the same time, small commercial enterprises sprout on every possible spot in every possible street, attached to buildings, to telephone poles, to electricity switching houses, or to anything else that does not move. These petty enterprises are by nature shelters, so many commercial stalls are, de facto, homes on the street for one or more people. The same is true of the kitchens of restaurants, parts of office buildings—indeed, any structure where a poor person has the smallest legitimate right to stay in or near a habitable structure, especially one that has water or a roof … In this setting, for the very poor, home is anywhere you can sleep.' (cited from http://www.columbia.edu/~rr322/UA-Mumbai.htm, last accessed in June 2012)

The middle class, also in need of land bought land on the city's periphery, often through illegal subdivisions. Subdivisions of agricultural land developed into informal residential settlements characterize the peri-urban areas of Indian cities. If private developers selling such plots have not obtained the necessary approval from the state, the layouts are considered 'unauthorized' though the extent of illegality/legality can vary. The above processes, in effect have created 'shadow cities', and 40 to 70 per cent of urban Indians live in such settlements that fall outside the purview of formal planning institutions and are mostly on the urban periphery.

The squatter settlements of the poor made of mud, thatch, and local discarded materials, of course, are to be distinguished from the unauthorized colonies of the middle class that are characterized by permanent residential and commercial buildings, two to three storeys high. But like the squatter settlements, the unauthorized colonies too do not have access to piped water supply, underground sewerage, and regular garbage collection, and must organize for these basic services on their own.

Squatter settlements or portions of them can get upgraded with time. Keeping a low profile in the early years, many of the occupants of squatter settlements have built permanent to semi-permanent structures and transformed their environment. Thus despite their illegality, squatter communities like the residents of unauthorized colonies have been contributing to the total housing stock and the economy of the city. With a huge hidden economy of their own, these areas have supported dense populations and many livelihoods via services, manufacturing units, and small businesses.

This brings us to an interesting aspect and it is the way the informal housing market is permitted to operate by the agencies and institutions of the formal city. For instance, while not being legal, it is allowed to exist with the backing of politicians looking for easy vote banks. Squatters and middle-class residents of unauthorized colonies will vote for any political candidate promising regularization of their settlement or promising to bring in water supply, sewerage, and electricity.

But going beyond this obvious connection between squatters and vote bank politics, is the view that the state gains from the existence of informality, particularly when it comes to issues of land. Due to the lack of proper land records and maps in most Indian cities, it is extremely difficult to know which plots are vested or owned by the government and this is more so on the metropolitan fringes. Land regulations are ambiguous and this ambiguity gives the state greater discretionary power in determining the use rights of the land and the extent of the legality/illegality of peri-urban land subdivisions. Residents of such areas thus face tenure-related uncertainties which the middle class are able to deal with through their residents' welfare associations that constantly seek to legalize their holdings and assert the legitimacy of their settlements using whatever means they can. The poor, on the other hand, unless backed by strong non-governmental organizations (NGOs) and civil society, experience eviction and displacement.

★ ★ ★

The complex cityscape of contemporary Indian cities is a product of both the processes of gentrification and informalization. The former is transforming older and particularly, former manufacturing sites into shopping centres, office complexes, and middle and upper income residential areas thereby extending the geographical area occupied by the well-to-do. The latter is responding to the needs of the poor and the middle class for living and working space in the city and its peripheries. What these processes mean for the social milieu of the city is explored in the next chapter.

5

Identity, Class, and Migration

What are Indian cities like as social entities? We now turn to this all-important question which is linked to the way individuals and communities see themselves and those different from them, their status in the social order, how they perceive public and private space, and what they do on a day-to-day basis that reproduces these mental and perceptual leanings. None of this has been static over time. In fact, it has been influenced by larger changes that the Indian society and economy have been undergoing since late colonial times as well as by the particularities of local-level conflicts and con-testations over rights to the city. This chapter highlights some important aspects of the social make-up of Indian cities and their influence in shaping the character of the city of the present. It necessitates a look at the changing basis of identity and class, which in turn determines who lives where in the city and how the pattern of residential differentiation is changing with time. It also means understanding the processes and types of migration into Indian cities and its impact on city life.

Changing Identity and Changing Basis of Residential Clusters

How people see themselves in the social context has an important bearing on the way they live and interact with others. In cities, this is especially important as the density of population is high and interaction with strangers or people different from oneself is a routine everyday matter. Often, because of the high densities and lack of space, one has to live in proximity to those perceived to be different from one. Up to the late colonial period, the primary bases for urban identity were criteria such as caste, mother tongue, religion, or inherited wealth. These criteria came with one's birth and did not reflect one's individual achievement, for instance, success in trade or in the professions.

With industrialization and modernity, achieved criteria began to be important in defining oneself. In developed countries, education and income became more important as social status markers and social status was directly reflected in where people lived in the city. A big question in the Indian context is in what ways is this transition from ascribed to achieved status happening and its spatial configurations.

In the contemporary Indian city, one of the simplest ways of gauging the social milieu is to look at who lives where and why. It leads us to questions such as: Do people of different ethnicities and religions live in distinct and segregated areas or is there a mixing of people in residential neighbourhoods? Where do the rich and poor live? Is socio-economic status the most important axis of separation between urban residents or is it still something more ascribed by birth like religion, caste, or language?

India's pluralistic and syncretic cultural past and the secular values of the Nehruvian state in the early decades after independence allowed for the coexistence of many layers of diversity within the urban social fabric. Residential clusters based on religious identity, language, caste, and occupation have coexisted within the city from pre-colonial times but over the last two centuries the relative importance of each of these and the way they intersect with class or economic criteria has changed.

During late colonial times, the movement of people from rural areas to towns and cities was critical to overcoming labour shortages in mills and factories and to providing a range of services. These rural migrants slowly adjusted to the city and made it their home. They brought along their ways of living and cultural practices and lived close to each other in tenement housing or chawls provided by the factory or in rented huts in slums close to their workplace. Those of the same caste or speaking the same language and/or practising the same religion settled close to each other. The cities were then a mosaic of neighbourhoods differentiated by caste, language, and/or religion.

Census data for Mumbai indicate that in 1881, the main basis for residential differentiation was ethnicity with Europeans, Muslims, and Parsees occupying distinct enclaves in south Mumbai. About 1930, a transition is noticeable with the clustering of Parsees giving way to Parsi–Christian areas. By 1961, the change is complete with socioeconomic status the main explanatory factor. Ethnicity is no longer the leading basis for why people choose where to live in the city and has been superseded by income and occupation. There was, however, one exception, and that was the Muslims who continued to live where they did in 1931, namely, in the areas of Chakla, Umarkhadi, Kahara Talao, and Second Nagpada in south Mumbai. While other ethnic groups such as the Parsees dispersed to other parts of the city away from the original urban core, Muslims remained where they were three decades ago and these were also the oldest parts of the city.

Mumbai's experience of the shift from an ethno-lingual-based residential clustering to an income-based one is not necessarily replicated with the same time-frame in other Indian cities. Mumbai also shows a much lower level of segregation based on caste. A comparative study of the seven leading Indian cities with 2001 census data has revealed that the Scheduled Caste (SC) and Scheduled Tribe (ST) populations within these cities show residential segregation of varying degrees, the highest being for Kolkata, Delhi, and Ahmedabad, lower levels for Hyderabad and Mumbai, and medium levels for Chennai and Bengaluru. In fact, in the older parts of the city, in its historic neighbourhoods near the core and surrounding wards, residential differentiation based on ascribed characteristics is still discernible in most Indian cities.

Kolkata, in particular, continues to show residential areas marked by ethnic, linguistic, and caste-based clustering. The latter, to a large extent, overlaps with very low income and low levels of literacy. Historically, the city experienced labour migration from the neighbouring states of Bihar and Orissa as well the migration of traders from Rajasthan, and there were distinct neighbourhoods of these groups, for instance, Urepara in Bhowanipur, and they have persisted for a much longer time. Hence the anthropologist N.K. Bose surveying Kolkata in the mid-1960s, called it a 'premature metropolis', one that was closer to a rural area in terms of the importance of affective ties. It is the only Indian city with a Chinatown, a Chinese enclave in the eastern part of the city with a small Chinese population who mainly run restaurants. However, over time, such ethnic enclaves are losing their distinctiveness due to the out-migration and emigration of the main ethnic group, in this case the Chinese. Likewise Anglo-Indian enclaves in parts of the city such as at Bow Bazaar are almost gone. Since the 1960s, the trend has been that of gradual merging with the rest of the city, but again, with some exceptions such as the Muslim enclaves and smaller enclaves of non-Bengali speakers scattered in the older wards of the city and within slums. In fact, Kolkata slums show a high degree of residential segregation within them with Bengali and non-Bengali speakers occupying distinct spaces with sharp boundaries and little social interaction.

While the relatively high level of residential seg-regation based on mother tongue and birthplace as found in Kolkata may be on the decline elsewhere, Muslim enclaves or concentrations of Muslims in poor and congested parts of the city remain a distinct and dark feature of the social milieu of most contemporary Indian cities. Here the minority population lives in a world of its own. The history of the recent past of several cities, however, reveals that this was not always the case, as in Hyderabad. In 1951, in the old walled city of Hyderabad, immediately after the dismantling of the Nizam's domain, although Muslims formed the majority community comprising 69 per cent, Hindus constituted 25 per cent and the rest or 5 per cent was made up of Jains, Christians, Sikhs, Buddhists, and others. The feudal court had required the services of skilled Muslim artisans, Kayasthas and Khatris for

administration, Bohra businessmen, Marwari merchants, and even SCs and STs. These different communities employed in the walled city had lived alongside
each other for centuries. But after the 1950s, there
was outmigration of upper-class Muslims, mainly to
Pakistan and also of all other non-Muslim groups side
by side with the in-migration of poorer Muslims. By
1981, the socioeconomic character of the walled city
had changed from a culturally dynamic and syncretic
place to an ethnic place, dominated by the poor of
one community.

In Kolkata, the Muslim population is highly concentrated in a few wards of the city as shown in Figure
8. These wards are either 'slum wards' where 90 per
cent of the population is living in slums as in Topsia,
Beniapukur, Tiljala, and Tangra in the eastern part
of the city or wards in old central Kolkata around
Nakhoda mosque and Tiretta Bazar, an overcrowded
and blighted area characterized by narrow lanes, crum-
bling housing, and little sign of buoyant real estate
development. This area is not a declared a slum but
is characterized by dilapidated housing, overloaded
infrastructure, high congestion, and an old settled
population that is downwardly mobile. A third area of

high Muslim concentration is Metiabruz and Garden Reach, on the western river front. Literacy levels are generally lower than the metropolitan average, particularly for women. High male unemployment and lack of jobs in the upwardly mobile professions is also a striking feature of these areas. Most residents work in the informal sector making Hawaii chappals (rubber slippers) or recycling waste, in small makeshift units. Drug addiction is a common sight in Topsia. A deep sense of marginalization and lack of empowerment comes through in conversations with residents. If such is the situation in a city governed by Left political parties for the last thirty-three years with an avowed policy of secularism, the situation of Muslims in other cities could hardly be better.

The continued existence of Muslim-dominated enclaves within the larger city points to a kind of entrenched socio-spatial exclusion that is tied in with the politics of the nation which has been characterized by sporadic communal disturbances post-independence and major communal disturbances post 1991, namely, the destruction of the Babri Masjid in 1992 and the Gujarat riots in 2002. Such outbreaks of violence have increased the fears of the minority community

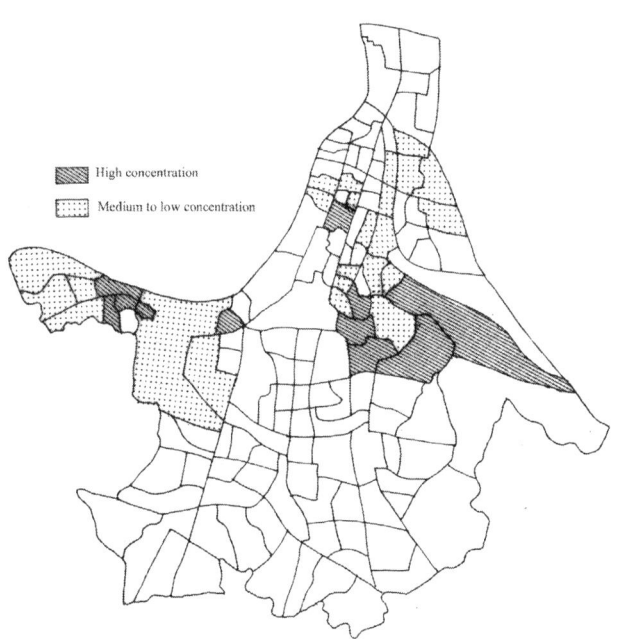

FIGURE 8   Predominant areas of Muslim concentration in the Kolkata Municipal Corporation, 2001
Source: Based on N.K. Bose's survey of 1964 (Bose 1968) and fieldwork in 2001.

who live close to each other for reasons of security. In Ahmedabad, new urban ghettos formed after the riots that reflected the mistrust of both Hindus and Muslims of each other. Residential areas developed very sharp boundaries as the two communities left former mixed areas and sought their own kind.

In contemporary Indian cities, Muslim-dominated areas indicate deprivation in multiple ways—economic, social, political, and cultural. Multiple deprivations, a term used in the social sciences, are characterized by several kinds of correlated and crosscutting deprivations which often compound one another. Its net effect is one of economic stagnation, disempowerment, and hopelessness.

For the country as a whole, post-independence, ideas of citizenship and right to the city have been slowly changing with the continued communalization of politics where political parties are divided along religious lines and engage in competitive politics. Non-religious and so-called secular parties also engage in communalization when a particular community is regarded as a vote bank and must be placated. The rise of sectarian political parties such as the BJP (Bharatiya Janata Party) and the Shiv Sena since the late 1960s have made these practices even more intense as the arena for many of their programmes and actions has been the city.

No city exemplifies this tendency better than Mumbai, India's financial capital. Its inbuilt inequalities and contradictions inherited from colonial times saw gradual unravelling post-independence as one of its recognized characteristics, that of being a cosmopolitan and liberal city started to change making it a sectarian, violence-prone, and sons-of-the-soil-driven city in the last two decades. If Mumbai's transition occurs in other cities, then the legacy of cultural pluralism that is still seen in many manifestations in the urban built environment will remain so only at the level of physical structures, inherited from the past. It will not be able to renew itself in future generations of urban residents as it fades out in day-to-day living practices.

Income as Differentiator

Other than the distinct separation of Muslims and their easily recognizable concentrations, religious and linguistic ethnicity as the basis for residential choice has been weakening in large cities. In fact, since the 1960s, the importance of income as a differentiator of social status and residential location has steadily increased and residential neighbourhoods based on income are easily discernible. At the extreme ends are the squatter settlements and slums of the poor and the upscale gated communities and bungalows and town-houses of the rich. But there are considerable stretches of the city that are neither slum nor upper income. These in-between residential areas are where the old middle class resides. Middle-income neighbourhoods show considerable heterogeneity in their origins and evolution but their common unifier is the presence of a more educated population with white collar jobs in the professions, government services, and local business and commerce.

Middle class residential areas are to be found in all Indian cities although many are undergoing gradual transformation to higher income neighbourhoods. In the port cities of Kolkata and Mumbai, older middle class neighbourhoods can trace their origins to the colonial period when they were developed on the outer margins of the fort, civil lines, and military cantonment. Some developed as residential areas of prosperous Indians but over time became more middle class. Others such as Hastings, in western Kolkata which originated as a shanty town for the labourers who constructed Fort William but later on changed in social composition, had a reverse trend. In fact, the original name of Hastings in maps dating back to

1841 was Coolie Bazaar but by 1868 it was already transforming, becoming an area of residence of retired Europeans. Today it is an upper middle-class area, the residence of army and navy officers and staff. Outside the fort, in the native or 'black town' middle-class localities emerged as sections were rebuilt along grid lines with proper roads, sanitation, and sewerage facilities. The Lottery Commission (1817) and its successor, the Lottery Committee (1836) opened up the native parts of old Kolkata through the creation of several north–south roads along with parks and public institutions. The activities of the Kolkata Improvement Trust, set up in 1912, further extended the level of civic services within municipal boundaries such that, aside from the inner city slums, much of the older parts of the city are today lower middle class to middle-middle class with housing that is six to seven decades old.

Post-independence, there was a huge demand for urban housing throughout the country, partly due to the natural increase in population, but also due to migration of refugees from the Partition and in-migration from rural areas. Many cities expanded both haphazardly and via new residential layouts and there was a flurry of construction activities by the state and private plot holders on government-allocated plots that catered to the housing needs of Partition refugees, government workers, middle-class professionals, and small business persons. Many private firms also built housing for their employees and to have a job in the formal sector had the added advantage of housing availability even in crowded cities. Housing type within middle-class neighbourhoods was either ownership homes or apartments in two to three-storey modern structures, often built through housing cooperatives, which in the last few decades have been raised to four and five storeys. In addition to these legal and approved housing units, there has been a growth of middle-class housing that is illegal or unauthorized and this has been typical of a city such as Delhi which saw many such units built outside the Master Plan. In fact, it has been estimated that about a third of Delhi's housing is unauthorized. In addition, middle class residential areas, approved by the authorities, have developed in a haphazard way along the fringes of cities. These are legal but very often lack proper road connectivity and water supply.

Middle-class neighbourhoods, in the Indian context, are different from those of the West in several ways.

Here income and class are very deeply intertwined with caste and this pattern has remained strong even in recent decades. Anthropological studies done in the late 1990s and early 2000s, in old and established urban neighbourhoods of various large cities reveal the close overlap between caste and class with the upper and middle classes predominantly comprising Brahmins, Kshatriyas, and Vaisyas and the lowest class being mainly made up of SCs/Dalits or STs. As SCs and STs are among the poorest residents, their residential concentration within the city's slums is high and their residential segregation is highly correlated with their economic condition. Table 12 shows the high level of poverty within these groups as compared to the general population. In 1999–2000, NSS data as given in Table 12 reveal that for towns of all size classes, the head count ratio of poverty (HCR) was significantly higher among SCs and STs as compared with the general population. In fact, in cities with a population of 1 million and above, while 13.7 per cent of the general population was living below the poverty line, for the STs and the SCs it was 27.2 per cent and 34 per cent, respectively.

TABLE 12 Concentration of Urban Poverty in the Lowest Social Groups

1999–2000	STs in urban pop. (%)	HCR for STs	SCs in urban pop. (%)	HCR for SCs	HCR for general population
Small towns (< 50,000)	5.1	40.4	16.2	49.8	32.0
Medium towns (50,000–1,000,000)	3.2	41.3	13.9	37.8	21.0
Large towns (1,000,000 & above)	1.8	27.2	13.0	34.0	13.7
All urban areas	3.4	38.9	14.4	40.9	22.1

Source: NSS data cited from Himangshu (2007).

Note: HCR = head count ratio of poverty.

Although the presence of successful entrepreneurs and professionals of lower caste is not unknown in upper and middle income housing complexes, by and large, the lowest social groups remain under-represented. On the other hand, they are disproportionately represented in slums as shown in Table 13 which highlights the issue for eight major Indian cities. It is based on the *National Family Health Survey* of 2005–6 (*NFHS-3*). Poor households are defined here as those in the lowest quartile of wealth.

TABLE 13 Percentage of SC/ST Households in Slums, Non-slums, and in the Poorest Quartile in Eight Major Indian Cities, 2005–6

Cities	SC/ST households in the general population	Slum	Non-slum	Poor
Delhi	18	38	13	39
Meerut	16.6	26	10	31
Kolkata	11.7	14	11	25
Indore	18.0	28	15	51
Mumbai	12.7	13	13	15
Nagpur	26.2	36	21	30
Hyderabad	13.8	17	13	32
Chennai	19.7	36	16	43

Source: Gupta et al. (2009: 78, Table 2.5).

In Table 13 we see interesting variations among the eight cities, with Mumbai showing a relatively low concentration of SC/STs in slums and in the poorest households as compared to their percentage in the general population. Delhi and Chennai, on the other hand, show quite an intense concentration of SC/STs both as slum-dwellers and as the poorest. In the case of Delhi, even as late as the mid-1990s, several 'Harijan bastis' exclusively housing the SCs existed in the metropolitan area under various names such as 'Harijan basti/colony, sweeper colony, Balmiki basti/colony, and Dr Ambedkar colony/nagar.

Geographically, the two types of settlement, slum and non-slum could occur side by side. Often, there is an old slum located in the middle of a higher income neighbourhood or the opposite, a middle-income neighbourhood surrounded by slums on all sides. In fact, even posh neighbourhoods can contain a cluster of huts or flimsy informal housing where domestic and lower class workers live. Thus different socioeconomic groups live in close proximity to one another but their social distance is high.

Another important distinction from residential areas in Western cities is that residential zoning is not that strict and land uses are mixed with both residential and commercial uses existing side by side. Most middle-income areas are served by a nearby market or bazaar and the ground floors of residential buildings are rented out to services and small businesses. Day care units, beauty salons, dressmaking, and private tuitions are often thriving from within middle-class homes. An informal sector operates alongside offering a range of goods and services from the small shops selling biscuits and cigarettes tucked away in a corner to vegetable and fruit sellers moving from lane to lane with their carts as in cities such as Mumbai. Informal service providers such as the dhobi (laundryman), newspaper boy, milk supplier, bottled water supplier, and various repair persons come door to door.

Like middle class residential areas, there is considerable heterogeneity within urban slums in India, ranging from abysmal conditions to the fairly tolerable and even upwardly improving. According to Census 2001, 42.6 million people or 23 per cent of India's total urban population lived in slums and this population is growing at a faster rate than the general population. But according to the Planning Commission's estimates of poverty, in 2004–5, at the national level, there were 80 million people in urban areas who fell below the poverty line. What this clearly indicates is that all of the urban poor are not living in slums. There are a significant number of poor people who live outside slums and this varies from city to city. On the basis of data from the *NFHS-3* survey cited earlier, Table 14 highlights this for eight metropolitan cities.

TABLE 14   Proportion of Slum Households to Total Households and Households in Slum and Non-slum Areas Who are Poor, 2005–6

Cities	Proportion of slum households to total households	% of poor households in slums	% of poor households in non-slums
Delhi	20	42	5
Meerut	43	23	10
Kolkata	33	23	8
Indore	20	9	12
Mumbai	56	10	3
Nagpur	34	29	15
Hyderabad	18	17	11
Chennai	18	32	12

Source: Gupta et al. (2009).

Table 14 shows the high proportion of households living in slums in major cities of the country and in fact, more than half of Mumbai's households live in slums. But while the proportion of households in the lowest quartile of wealth is much higher in slums as compared to that outside slums, the table clearly indicates that there are also poor households living outside slums and this percentage varies from 3 per cent in Mumbai to 15 per cent in Nagpur. What it also reveals is that in Mumbai while 56 per cent of the households live in slums, they are not necessarily very poor as only 10 per cent of slum households fell in the lowest quartile of wealth. Much of Mumbai's slum living is more a crisis of housing than a crisis of income and employment. But for the cities of Meerut, Kolkata, Nagpur, and Chennai, slums do contain a high proportion of poor households.

Within slums, a distinction has to be made between notified slums and non-notified slums. Notified slums are generally older and more permanent. They have been recognized by the local government and thus have better access to basic amenities. Non-notified slums are the 'unauthorized/unregistered' slums and squatter settlements that have the worst living conditions. In 2005, the Kolkata Municipal Corporation estimated its slum population to be 1,675,476, and living in 5,072 registered slums in 141 wards of the city. Slums comprised 31 sq. km or 18 per cent of the city's total area of 187.33 sq. km. But these figures of slum population and slum clusters are both underestimates. The Corporation's own Development Report of 2007 admits that there are 'equal or more' numbers of unauthorized/unregistered slums.

While slums in the largest cities are well-known phenomena, their presence brought to the forefront of popular consciousness via the news media and films such as *Slumdog Millionaire*, smaller cities and large towns too have a growing slum problem. Table 15 shows the distribution of the slum population by city size in 2001.

TABLE 15   Distribution of Slum Population by City Size, 2001

City/Town size	Number of cities and towns	Slum population (in million)	% of total slum population
>4 million	5	11.06	26.0
2–4 million	8	3.76	8.8
1–2 million	14	2.88	6.8
500,000 to 1 million	42	5.81	13.7
Total	69	23.51	55.3
100,000 to 500,000	309	13.94	32.7
Total Class I towns		37.45	88

Source: Census of India, 2001, cited from Mathur (2009: 20, Table 13).

Interesting to note is the fact that medium-sized cities with a population of less than 1 million to 500,000 accounted for around 14 per cent of the total slum population and small cities with a population of between 100,000 and 500,000 accounted for 33 per cent or a third. The land and housing crisis of the metropolitan cities is clearly becoming a feature of smaller cities as well.

However, the growth of the slum population does not necessarily mean growth in slum acreage within the city. In fact, post liberalization, one noticeable trend in several of the largest metropolitan cities has been the declining amount of land available for slums. This has happened due to increasing slum demolitions and slum removal as the land upon which they exist is regarded as costly and in great demand by developers. The effect of increasing slum demolitions has been an increase in overcrowding and less availability of cheap rental housing for the poor at locations close to their workplaces. While the growing prosperity of the urban middle class is increasing their demand for the services of maids, cooks, and drivers, the city has less and less places where they can afford to live. Thus the promise of jobs in India's cities has been occurring side by side with less affordable housing. Yet, in the last decade, more people migrated to Indian cities than ever before. What does this mean for Indian cities?

Migration

Migration has always played an important role in the growth of cities; so too in Indian cities. But the attractiveness of different parts of the country to migrants and the cities therein has varied considerably. It has also varied by city size with metropolitan cities having been far more attractive as compared to smaller cities and towns.

Historically, the Indian population has been characterized by low mobility, even after independence and the onset of modernization and nationalist planning. But over the last decade, rural to urban migration has picked up, particularly, in the western states of the country. During 1991–2001, short-distance or intra-state rural to urban migration saw the movement of 14.2 million people to urban areas while long-distance or inter-state rural to urban migration added another 6.3 million. Both these kinds of migration were greater than in the previous decade, their growth rate being 7.3 per cent and 76.5 per cent, respectively. Subtracting the numbers of people who left urban areas for rural areas, the net gain by urban areas was around 14 million. This is considerably higher than the net gain during the 1970s and 1980s when it was 9.3 million and 10.6 million, respectively. What the Census 2001 migration data also reveal is the growing importance of urban-to-urban migration. Although this does not result in any net addition to the urban population, it implies a redistribution of population within urban areas and can reveal people's perceptions of educational opportunities, trade-offs in quality of life, and availability of jobs requiring specialized skills. Both short-distance and long-distance urban-to-urban migration grew significantly during 1991–2001 at 23.6 per cent and 24.3 per cent, respectively, and involved a total of 14.2 million people.

Of the different kinds of migration streams, one of the most interesting is the long-distance or inter-state rural to urban migration stream. It is dominated by male migrants moving from one state to another in search of better economic opportunities. The origin or the sending-out areas and the destination or receiving areas of the migrants are thus a good index of which parts of the country are doing well and the reverse. Figure 9 presents the major inter-state long distance flows during 1991–2001.

What is instantly observable is the huge outflow from UP to Maharashtra, Gujarat, Delhi, Haryana, Punjab,

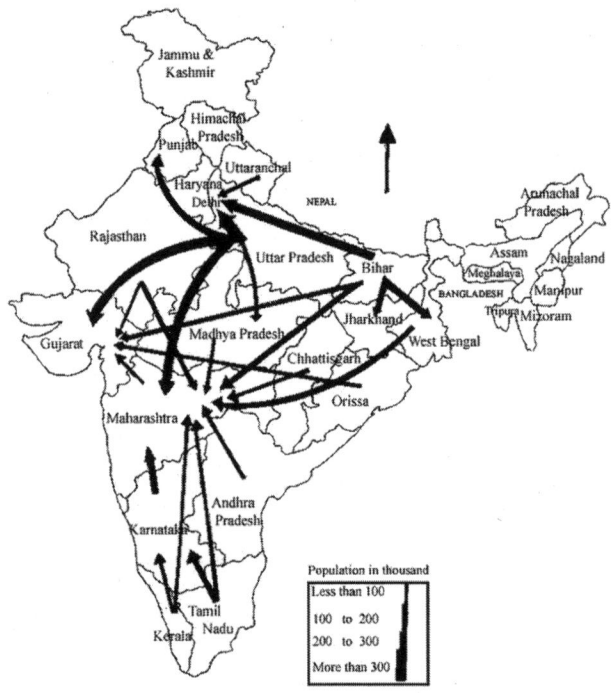

FIGURE 9   Inter-state rural–urban migration, 2001
Source: Based on Bhagat and Mohanty (2009).

and Madhya Pradesh. Uttar Pradesh experienced a net
loss of 2.7 million people during 1991–2001. This is
part of a pattern of out-migration that has been happening since the 1980s. During the period 1986–91,

UP had a net loss of 911,000 migrants, exporting people to almost every large state. Another important exporter is Bihar which sent out 1.7 million people during 1991–2001. For Bihari migrants, the main destination was Delhi, followed by West Bengal and Maharashtra. A second feature is the magnetic pull of Maharashtra which experienced a net gain of 3.2 million migrants in 1991–2001. During 1986–91, Maharashtra had attracted 475,000 migrants many of whom headed for the Mumbai metropolitan region. This urban region and Maharashtra, in general, received migrants from all over the country. A third feature is the continuing attraction of the Delhi/Haryana area which received 475,000 migrants during 1986–91 and then 1.7 million during 1991–2001. Finally, a destination of emerging importance is Gujarat with a net migration of 247,000 during 1986–91 and around 670,000 during 1991–2001. It is the only state to which Maharashtra has lost a substantial number of people during the fifteen years extending from 1986 to 2001.

Figure 9 clearly shows the most preferred states by long-distance migrants as well as their home states. Other than the cities of Mumbai and Delhi around which two distinct regional migration systems have evolved, what other cities within the leading receiving states are also attractive to migrants? This can be inferred from the percentage of migrants to the total population of different cities as shown in Table 16.

TABLE 16   Percentage of Lifetime Migrants to Total Population in Major Cities of the Leading Destination States/Areas, 1971–2001

State/City	UA/MC	2001	1991	1981	1971
Maharashtra					
Greater Mumbai	UA	43.6	35.2	51.5	56.9
Pune	UA	44.6	27.5	48.4	48.7
Nagpur	UA	30.5	18.2	34.9	36.8
Nashik	UA	50.1			
Gujarat					
Ahmedabad	UA	33.7	33.7	37.9	44.2
Surat	UA	57.6	48.7	29.4	
Vadodara	UA	43.0	42.8		
Rajkot	UA	41.4			
Delhi region/north					
Delhi	UA	43.4	39.1	44.6	51.7
Faridabad	MC	55.4			
Ludhiana	MC	57.1			

Source: Census of India, 1971–2001, Migration Tables, cited from Singh (2009: 61, Table 3.10).

Note: UA—urban agglomeration; MC—municipal corporation.

All the cities shown in Table 16 have a much higher proportion of migrants to total population than the

Indian urban average. Among the largest cities in the country, Mumbai and Delhi continue to be net receiving areas, although in the case of both cities, the percentage of migrants to total population has actually fallen since the 1970s. In Ahmedabad too, the percentage of migrants to total population has been dropping while it is has been growing in Gujarat's smaller metropolitan areas such as Surat and Vadodara. Likewise, Faridabad and Ludhiana, both small metropolitan areas with a population of 1.05 million and 1.39 million, respectively, have been growing very fast, largely due to migration. In both cities, more than half the population is made up of migrants. Together with Surat, these cities have the highest proportion of migrants to total city population in the country. Surat's diamond-cutting industry is heavily dependent on out-of-state migrants. Interestingly, the south which has seen considerable economic growth post liberalization has not been as attractive to migration from other states. Table 17 shows the percentage of lifetime migrants in the total population of some of the major cities in the south.

What is noticeable from Table 17 is that Bengaluru and Vishakhapatnam, both relatively fast-growing cities, have the highest percentages of migrants among major

TABLE 17   Percentage of Lifetime Migrants in the Major Cities
of South India, 1991–2001

State/City	UA/MC	2001	1991	1981	1971
Tamil Nadu					
Chennai	UA	25.0	27.6	34.5	36.7
Coimbatore	UA	21.9	27.7		
Madurai	UA	18.3	25.3		
Andhra Pradesh					
Hyderabad	UA	26.1	25.9	21.0	22.8
Vishakhapatnam	UA	37.6	42.3		
Vijayawada	UA	30.1			
Karnataka					
Bengaluru	UA	36.7	28.7	37.6	37.7
Kerala					
Kochi	UA	30.2	24.9		

Source: Census of India, 1971–2001, Migration Tables, cited from
Singh (2009: 61, Table 3.10).
Note: UA—urban agglomeration; MC—municipal corporation.

cities of the south but these percentages are still lower
than those of the dynamic cities of the west and the
capital region. Also to be noted is how Hyderabad's
proportion of lifetime migrants has been slowly rising
while that of Chennai has been steadily declining since
the 1970s.

What about major cities in the 'sending out' states
of UP and Bihar? While long-distance migration to
these cities would be negligible, as leading regional

urban centres, do they experience some migration from surrounding or nearby areas? This is indicated in Table 18. As expected, we see a much lower proportion of migrants in the total population. Apart from the capital cities of Lucknow and Patna, it is 20 per cent and less for the major cities of these states. Several of these cities such as Kanpur, Lucknow, and Allahabad had a more mixed population, both ethnically as well as in terms of migrant-local presence in the aftermath of independence but, over the following decades there has been net outmigration of these groups.

TABLE 18 Percentage of Lifetime Migrants to Total Population in Major Cities of Sending-out States, 1991–2001

State/City	UA/MC	2001	1991	1981	1971
Uttar Pradesh					
Kanpur	UA	19.4	19.7	29.4	37.0
Lucknow	UA	27.8	27.9	27.4	33.5
Agra	UA	12.0			
Varanasi	UA	16.7	7.2		
Meerut	UA	20.1			
Allahabad	UA	14.3			
Bihar					
Patna	UA	26.7			

Source: Census of India, 1971–2001, Migration Tables, cited from Singh (2009: 61, Table 3.10).
Note: UA—urban agglomeration; MC—municipal corporation.

Given the size of India's urban population which was 286 million in 2001, a net gain from rural migration of 14 million in the 1990s, while being an improvement over the decade of the 1970s and 1980s, is still rather low. Of this only around 5.3 million involved crossing state boundaries. This is not a large number taking the country as a whole, but because the destinations of out-of-state migrants are primarily three or four economically dynamic states, the in-migration stream to these chosen states is not insignificant. Thus, despite relatively small numbers for a country the size of India, politically, it is inter-state migration that has become a sensitive issue with sons-of-the-soil backlashes in states such as Maharashtra. Spearheaded by the Shiv Sena and its splinter, the Maharashtra Navnirman Sena, Mumbai witnessed hostile and violent actions against north Indians, namely, people from Uttar Pradesh and Bihar. The sectarian backlash against migrants has sent out negative signals and is contrary to the spirit of openness and hospitality to strangers. It has primarily affected the bottom end of the social strata, people leaving their home areas out of economic distress and seeking menial or low-end jobs in the city or self-employment in the informal sector.

But this is not the whole story of urban migration for, at the same time, a great churning is also happening as the Indian city provides opportunities for upward mobility through migration and the availability of better educational opportunities and jobs, particularly in the service sector. Post liberalization, modern low to middle-status occupations in hospitals, airlines, hotels, and beauty parlours or salons have generated unique migration streams of lower middle class young women moving from semi-rural and small-town India to large metropolitan cities and transforming the lives of both themselves and their families. For the young seeking higher status jobs, moving for higher education opportunities has also become a significant trend in the last decade. These are often urban-to-urban movements, for instance, from Kolkata to Bengaluru to join private engineering and medical colleges or the all-India urban rush to the city of Kota in Rajasthan to prepare for the Indian Institute of Technology (IIT)/medical entrance exams.

These examples point to the gradual emergence of a national higher education market and along with it a labour market for highly skilled and specialized jobs with high human capital endowments that have linked the country and its urban areas in new ways. Even remote parts of the country have been caught in the sweep of this yearning for upward mobility as seen in the increasing out-migration from the north-eastern states to the plains of India, and in particular, to the states of West Bengal, Bihar, and Uttar Pradesh and to cities such as Kolkata, Bengaluru, and Delhi, primarily for jobs but also for higher studies. The personal success of individuals from the north-east in sports and entertainment and their greater visibility in the popular media has been an added spur to leave the region and look for opportunities in mainstream India. In fact, in many parts of the north-east, rural areas face a labour shortage and some of this shortage is being overcome with temporary workers from Bangladesh.

Rural and Peri-urban Labour Supply for Low-end Jobs

While migration as a process of population movement into and out of cities has been an important contributor to the social and economic composition of cities, there are other temporary and shorter-duration movements in and out of the city that are also important but not captured in official Indian data sources. Migration data in India whether collected by the Census or the NSSO do not contain any information on day-to-day movements in and out of cities for work. Yet such movements have increased in number and frequency with improvements and extensions in bus, metro, and rail transportation systems in the larger cities. Cities such as Kolkata and Mumbai receive over a million workers each working day and their presence in the city affects the social milieu in several ways. One is through a regaining of gender balance as a high proportion of commuters are women entering the city for domestic work. Like the long-term migrants, these women too are from poor socioeconomic backgrounds coming to the city to supplement family income through work as maids and cooks in middle class homes. They live in villages or in peri-urban areas adjacent to the city. Apart from the hard work at relatively cheap rates, rural and semi-urban commuters bring to the city their rural-based value systems and expectations of paternalistic treatment in the workplace. The workers in turn are affected by what they do and experience in the city carrying back into their villages not only their monthly earnings but also a bit of the urban way of life.

Thus the city's influence extends far beyond its actual boundaries.

Commuting from rural and peri-urban areas also involves males, mostly working in the informal sector, for instance, in garages and small workshops in the city. If there is work in the formal sector, it is mostly on contract basis, for instance, as lift men, security guards, and now even as store attendants. In fact, a leading hyper-mart of Kolkata, Spencer's Retail, buses in its workers from outside the city.

★ ★ ★

The social milieu of Indian cities is experiencing both continuity and change. We see this in the way city dwellers view themselves and others. While on the one hand, the socio-spatial exclusion of the historically disadvantaged continues to remain a feature of the contemporary Indian city, on the other hand, new patterns of mobility and migration are loosening the grip of old constraints and widening social opportunities for some. The latter includes educated or skilled migrants from outside, both out-of-state migrants and rural migrants from within the state.

Identity based on attributes inherited from birth such as mother tongue, birthplace, caste, and religion remains important for the poor and marginalized who continue to live in distinct clusters within slums and areas of poor housing and rundown infrastructure. The SCs and STs as well as Muslims fall into this category of the excluded and their exclusion is visible in their residential segregation. In middle-class areas, while education and white collar jobs are important for group identity, caste and class often intersect blurring their distinction as principles of differentiation. In the newer parts of the city or the metropolitan area, self-identity is increasingly determined by other criteria such as occupation, education and income, and residential clustering is based on socioeconomic status. Post liberalization, upper income residential areas are displaying a 'consumerist cosmopolitanism' shaped by access to lifestyle and material accessories that are global. More frequent overseas travel and the presence of relatives abroad and non-resident Indians (NRIs) in the city have added to this process. Strong determinants of who lives where in these upcoming and developing areas have been income and lifestyle. Quality of life or 'the good life' is of considerable importance to these residents. The next chapter takes up this issue, looking at both its potential and limits in an urban scenario of uneven access and scarce resources.

6

Quality of Life

As India's population is becoming more and more urban, the quality of life in its cities is receiving more attention from the popular media, business houses and corporations, as well as policymakers. Even politicians are incorporating aspects of it in their electoral strategies to gather urban votes. In this chapter we turn to this critically important issue and ask whether two decades of higher economic growth have improved the quality of life in Indian cities. But first we have to decide which components of quality of life to focus on, given that it is a very broad term covering a range of issues with little absolute agreement on what constitutes 'the good life'. However, by and large, it is understood to include all the basic needs of human beings such as water, food, clothing, and shelter as well as higher needs such as freedom of speech, political and artistic freedom, and peace and tranquillity. In a short book such as this, we will be limited to examining Indian cities in terms of the former and not venture into the latter. Thus the focus will be on the provision of basic services such as drinking water supply, sewerage, drainage, and garbage removal, and a few social goods such health facilities and education. As in the previous chapters, it will be necessary to discuss these issues keeping in mind the formal city of planned and permanent structures as well as the informal city of slums and squatter settlements.

Basic Urban Services

These cover the most fundamental aspects of quality of life and we begin by asking whether their condition in Indian cities is improving or getting worse with increasing population. This question can be partly answered by turning to the NSSO's periodic reports on housing conditions and amenities. The latest available report is for a survey done in the year 2008–9 (65th Round) with comparative data for earlier rounds conducted in 1993 and 2002. These three periods will give us a sense of the condition of basic facilities and housing and changes experienced post liberalization.

First, in the fifteen years between 1993 and 2008–9, urban India as a whole has made some progress in covering urban households with basic facilities such as drinking water availability, bathroom and toilet/latrine facilities, and electricity. Table 19 shows the changes.

TABLE 19 Percentage of Households with Access to Basic Facilities in Urban India, 1993, 2002, and 2008–9

Year	Drinking water from a tap	Bathroom facility	Toilet/Latrine facility	Electricity
1993	70	53	69	82
2002	73	68	82	92
2008–9	74	79	89	96

Source: NSS Report No. 535 (65th Round).

While both electricity and sanitary facilities have shown considerable improvement, the increase in coverage of urban households by tap water supply has been slow. However, detailed data reveal either some improvement in quality of the facility or less inconvenience in accessing the facility. For instance, in the case of drinking water, although coverage under tap water has increased very slowly, the percentage of households with water available in their premises has gone up significantly from 66 per cent in 1993 to 74.5 per cent in 2008–9. Regarding the sufficiency of the quantity of water available to urban households, in the latest period surveyed, it was found that 91 per cent of urban households received sufficient water throughout the year. Around 8–9 per cent did not receive sufficient drinking water during the month of May, the height of the summer. During the months of April to June around 5 per cent of urban households experienced water shortage.

Table 20 shows other indicators of the improvement in type and convenience of basic facilities over the fifteen-year period.

TABLE 20 Quality of Some Basic Facilities by Percentage of Urban Households Covered in 1993, 2002, and 2008–9

	Drinking water within premises of house	Attached bathroom	Septic tank/Flush toilet	Exclusive use of latrine facility
1993	66.2	27.5	58.1	40.4
2002	70.3	41.1	70.7	53.5
2008–9	74.5	48.0	77.3	58.1

Source: NSS Report No. 535 (65th Round).

Almost half the urban households, 48 per cent, had an attached bathroom in 2008–9, up from just

27 per cent in 1993. Around 77 per cent of them were using a flush toilet or septic tank facility in 2008–9, an increase of 21 per cent compared to 1993. Likewise, there has been an increasing trend in the exclusive use of a toilet facility. This has gone up from 40 per cent to 58 per cent. A third point to be noted is that there is a sharp improvement in the quality of the basic facilities with the rising economic status of the urban household. This is shown in Table 21.

TABLE 21 Access to Basic Facilities by Urban Households by Monthly Per Capita Expenditure (MPCE) Classes, 2008–9

MPCE quintile class (in Rs)	Exclusive use drinking water facility	Attached bathroom	Septic tank/ Flush latrine	No latrine	Exclusive use of latrine facility
0–20	28.5	19.1	48.6	33.3	34.3
20–40	35.5	30.1	66.1	19.8	46.8
40–60	43.2	41.1	76.2	9.8	55.7
60–80	52.0	53.9	85.6	3.6	64.0
80–100	66.3	75.7	94.4	.6	75.7
All urban	47.0	48.0	77.3	11.3	58.1

Source: NSS Report No. 535 (65th Round).

Drinking water for the sole use of the household increased from 28.5 per cent in the lowest quintile of monthly per capita expenditure (MPCE) to 66.3

per cent in the highest quintile. This means that two-thirds of the households in the highest quintile of MPCE have a drinking water source for exclusive use. The presence of an attached bathroom in the house increases even more sharply from 19.1 per cent for the lowest quintile to 75.7 per cent in the highest quintile. Likewise, septic tanks and the associated flush latrine are available to 94 per cent of those in the highest quintile of MPCE while having exclusive use of a toilet/latrine facility rises from 34 per cent in the lowest quintile to 76 per cent in the highest quintile. Table 21 also reveals the fact that a shocking 33 per cent or a third of those in the lowest expenditure class had no access to a toilet or latrine. It means that neither a shared latrine nor a public facility is available to them. On a daily basis, this is considerable inconvenience, loss of time searching for a proper place as well as loss of dignity having to use makeshift places and the roadside.

Thus while the overall progress made in basic facilities in urban India deserves recognition and this, despite the rising population, there still remains the major challenge of providing coverage to all urban residents including the very poor.

Housing Conditions and Quality

This is an important indicator of the quality of life, and improvement in housing conditions can greatly contribute to raising the standard of living of urban residents. Housing conditions would also include the state of the micro-environment surrounding the house, such as roads, drains, and so on, all of which have a big impact on neighbourhood quality. According to the NSS report of housing conditions in 2008–9, 91.7 per cent of urban households were living in *pucca* or solid structures, 6.2 per cent in semi-pucca structures, and only 2 per cent were in *kutcha* structures. This is indeed a vast improvement over the past as indicated in Table 22.

TABLE 22   Distribution of Urban Households by Type of Dwelling Unit

Urban All-India	Pucca	Semi-pucca	Kutcha
1993	73.8	17.9	8.3
2002	76.8	19.9	3.2
2008–9	91.7	6.2	2.1

Source: NSS, Report 535, 65th Round.

An interesting finding of the survey is that the predominant type of residential structure in India's urban areas continues to be the independent house. This refers to a stand-alone unit or a separate structure with its own entrance and self-contained arrangements. 'Others' refers to inferior accommodation and as can be seen from Table 23, this category declines with rising income. Another trend seen in Table 23 is the predominance of the flat/apartment with rising income and the greater prevalence of the independent house among those with lower income.

TABLE 23 Predominant Types of Housing in Urban India, 2008–9

MPCE	Independent house	Flat/Apartment	Others
0–20	66.4	11.8	21.6
20–40	67.8	13.0	19.2
40–60	63.4	18.5	18.1
60–80	56.8	24.1	19.2
80–100	44.9	43.0	12.1
All	58.1	24.4	17.4

Source: NSS, Report 535, 65th Round.

While these are averages for the urban areas of the entire country, it is likely that for the largest cities, the predominant dwelling unit is now the flat.

Moving on to the important issue of the condition of the housing structure, the NSS is able to report on only those houses inhabited by owners themselves.

Around 62 per cent of the total housing stock was found to be owner-occupied. The condition of the housing structure is affected by the age of the house with obsolescence marked by age 60. It was found that only 3 per cent of urban households live in dwellings over 60 years old and nearly 54 per cent of urban households lived in houses in good condition that did not need any repairs. Around 37 per cent were in houses that were in satisfactory condition that needed only minor repairs. But the remaining 8 per cent were living in houses in poor condition where immediate major repairs were required and without which the habitation was unsafe.

A critical aspect of the quality of housing is the amount of space provided to families, both in terms of the unit as a whole and also on a per person basis. While the per capita availability of living space is a modest 9 sq. m per person for urban areas as a whole, there is a big difference between what is available for the lowest quintile and the highest quintile. In fact, there is a trebling of per capita space in the highest quintile at 16.83 sq. m while at 5.63 sq. m per person, the per capita living space for the two lowest quintiles in the urban areas was actually lower than that available to the bottom two quintiles of the rural areas which was 5.84 sq. m and 6.84 sq. m, respectively. The difference between the lowest and highest quintiles in the rural areas was also less with just a doubling of per capita space in the highest quintile.

Quality of Immediate Neighbourhood

This refers to the areas immediately surrounding the house and in India their quality is still largely dependent on the presence/availability of proper drainage, garbage disposal and roads. A proper drainage system would refer to the 'easy' carrying off of waste water and liquid waste from the house without any overflow or seepage. All three facilities are essential for maintaining hygiene and cleanliness in the micro environment surrounding the house and while they are taken for granted in the cities of the developed countries, in urban India they still remain among its biggest challenges. Aggregate national data, however, does not fully reveal this, as for instance, according to the NSS, the proportion of urban households still exposed to open kutcha drains was only 5.8 per cent in 2008–9 while those without any drainage (kutcha or pucca) was

14.8 per cent. Garbage collection from urban households has also improved somewhat with 78.6 per cent of them reporting such a service, and only around 6 per cent of urban households reported not having direct access to a road.

Condition of Basic Services in Urban Slums

The NSS report provides a general picture of the state of basic facilities in urban areas in India and how some improvements have been occurring in the last fifteen years. But as is evident, the entire population of existing towns and cities is still not covered although coverage has been improving since the 1990s. The uncovered population would be the poorest people, mostly living in slums and squatter settlements and hence, to get a more realistic picture of the quality of life in Indian cities, it is necessary to examine conditions within slum areas separately. This is provided through another NSS report (Number 534) on a survey conducted in 2008–9 on urban slums.

Since the meaning of 'slum' varies in India according to the agency conducting the survey, it is necessary explain what the NSS means by slums and the fact that it classifies slums as 'notified ' and 'non-notified'. According to the NSS, a slum is 'a compact settlement with a collection of poorly built tenements, mostly of temporary nature, crowded together usually with inadequate sanitary and drinking water facilities in unhygienic conditions'. Such an area is considered a slum if it has at least twenty households living in that area. Notified slums, as mentioned in Chapter 4, refer to those slums that have been officially recognized as slums by the respective municipality, municipal corporation, or any other urban local body or by a development authority. Non-notified slums are those that have not received such recognition. Generally, notified slums are in a much better condition with regard to basic facilities as they are serviced by the urban local body. Since 1976–7, the NSS has been periodically carrying out all-India surveys of urban slums with surveys in 1993, 2002, and 2008–9. Through these surveys it is possible to see if any changes are occurring in slums and squatter settlements and what kinds of changes.

One of the first observations to be noted in the latest survey of urban slums is that, for the country as a whole, the estimated numbers of slums have decreased from 56,311 in 1993 to 51,688 in 2002 and 48,994 in 2008–9. Some experts explain this as the result of increased slum demolitions, post liberalization. Second, around 50 per cent of urban slums are notified and 50 per cent are not notified and this has been so both in 2002 as well as in 2008–9. However, in states such as Delhi, Uttar Pradesh, and Orissa, notified slums comprised only 32–34 per cent of the total, while in Andhra Pradesh they comprised 75 per cent of the total.

Turning to the condition of housing in slums, the report indicates some improvement in the quality of housing. In 2002, the percentage of slums in which the majority of houses were pucca was 48 per cent. By 2009, this had increased to 57 per cent. Households within 64 per cent of the notified slums lived mainly in pucca structures as compared to 50 per cent in the non-notified slums. Thus there has been a gradual increase in permanent structures within slums and decrease in the kinetic element. Improvements have also been made in terms of latrine availability with the percentage of slums with no latrines falling from 17 per cent in 2002 to 10 per cent in 2008 although there are some states with abysmally low levels for both notified and non-notified slums such as Orissa (49 and 36 per cent) and two better-off states, Gujarat (39 and 48 per cent), and Tamil Nadu (27 and 40 per cent). Garbage pick-up has also increased with the percentage of notified slums not having the service falling from 16 to 10 per cent and that of non-notified slums from 46 to 23 per cent.

However, on several other dimensions, what is noticeable in the comparison of slum conditions between 2002 and 2008 is that the extension of the basic infrastructure network has stagnated and even declined. For instance, in the case of electricity, in 2002 while in 84 per cent of notified slums electricity was available for both households and street, in 2008, this had declined to 76 per cent. For non-notified slums, the figure remained at 53 per cent for both years. Regarding sewerage and drainage, while notified slums without drainage have declined from 15 to 10 per cent and non-notified from 44 to 23 per cent, the decline has been due to the creation of open drains. Underground or covered drainage has increased marginally from 25 to 39 per cent in notified slums and from 13 to 24 per cent in non-notified slums.

Table 24 summarizes the percentage distribution of slums by change in slum facilities during the five years prior to 2008–9. Deterioration of facilities varying between 0 to 6 per cent in notified slums and 0 to 9 per cent in non-notified slums has not been included.

As can be seen, improvements have been uneven across different facilities but in general, they have been higher within notified as compared to non-notified slums. Clearly, much more remains to be done.

Who will do it? Despite the policy thrust promoting urban service delivery through multiple agencies and not just the state, it is interesting to note that the authority responsible for whatever improvements in basic facilities within slums that have taken place has been overwhelmingly the government. This is the case for both notified and non-notified slums. NGOs and residents have played a part in improvements in latrine facilities but regarding the rest of the facilities in Table 24, their role has been small.

City-level Differences between Slum and Non-slum Areas

From the all-India data provided by the NSS reports on urban slums, we will now turn to a report on the

TABLE 24 Percentage Distribution of Slums by Direction of Change in Condition of Specific Slum Facilities during the Last Five Years to 2008–9, All-India

Facility	Notified			Non-notified		
	Improved	Slum Did not change	Non-existent	Improved	Slum Did not change	Non-existent
Water supply	49	44	2	30	55	9
Electricity	38	59	0	29	61	9
Street light	43	44	10	29	49	21
Latrine	34	49	10	24	52	21
Drainage	40	45	11	28	45	23
Sewerage	23	53	19	11	50	38
Garbage disposal	42	44	8	26	46	23
Road within slum	53	44	2	30	63	3
Approach road	52	37	5	31	52	8

Source: NSS Report 534, Statement 15, p. 30.

health and living conditions in eight large Indian cities brought out by the Ministry of Family Health and Welfare in 2009. This gives us a useful indication of the city-level differences between slum and non-slum areas regarding the provision of basic services. The report is based on the *National Family Health Survey* of 2005–6 and covers the following eight cities: Chennai, Delhi, Hyderabad, Indore, Kolkata, Meerut, Mumbai, and Nagpur. Since not all the poor live in slums, the report provides information on the living conditions for slum areas, non-slum areas, and for the poorest quartile of households regardless of where they may be living. Some key aspects of the quality of life for these three groups are given in Table 25.

With the exception of Meerut, for all the other cities shown in Table 25 the availability of piped drinking water is not a problem for most urban households and the gap between slum and non-slum areas is small. In fact, in Chennai, a higher percentage in slum areas has access to it as compared to non-slum areas. For the poorest quartile, access is high in the cities of Chennai, Hyderabad, and Mumbai. But, regarding improved toilet facilities that are not shared but used exclusively by the household, all the eight cities have a long

TABLE 25 Key Aspects of Quality of Life in Census Slum and Non-slum Areas and among the Poorest Quartile, 2005–6

% households	Chennai	Delhi	Hyderabad	Indore	Kolkata	Meerut	Mumbai	Nagpur
Piped drinking water								
Slum	72	84	97	71	85	38	100	88
Non-slum	68	86	99	74	78	69	100	86
Poor	89	76	95	64	70	14	99	67
Improved toilet, not shared								
Slum	19	24	60	56	24	44	21	52
Non-slum	38	74	69	66	58	57	46	74
Poor	8	5	24	14	6	20	3	26
Five and more per sleeping room								
Slum	32	48	28	23	41	35	40	32
Non-slum	20	19	30	19	15	26	39	18
Poor	43	60	51	55	20	65	49	47
Using kerosene and solid fuels								
Slum	55	52	33	13	65	47	32	44
Non-slum	25	10	25	15	30	20	15	20
Poor	92	64	88	73	98	92	96	89

Source: Gupta et al. (2009).

way to go. Even in non-slum areas, the percentage of households with this kind of facility is moderate, the highest being in Delhi and Nagpur at 75 per cent. In slum areas, it is even lower. One exception is Hyderabad where 60 per cent of slum households have access to this type of a facility. In the poorest quartile, it is weakly present with the highest percentage being in Hyderabad and Nagpur.

The third indicator in Table 25 is the percentage of households that have five or more persons sleeping in a room. It is a measure of household congestion and overcrowding. What is interesting to note is that even non-slum areas have a certain amount of over-crowding and in the case of Mumbai, there is hardly any difference between slum and non-slum areas. Both are equally congested. In Kolkata, on the other hand, overcrowding among the poorest quartile is much less as compared to slum areas. This is because many poor households continue to reside in large old buildings as owners and tenants in the north and central locations of the city.

The final indicator in Table 25 gives us insights into another dimension of the quality of life and that is, the kind of fuel used for cooking and even lighting.

The use of kerosene and solid fuels that emit smoke is very high both in the slums and in the poorest quartile. Apart from Kolkata, non-slum areas in the other cities show the predominant use of liquefied petroleum gas (LPG) and other non-smoke-emitting fuels.

Health

Health facilities show the same kinds of disparities between the poor and the non-poor. Although urban India and particularly, the largest cities, have far superior health facilities as compared to rural areas, within urban areas there are significant differences in access by income class. This situation has been exacerbated by the poor quality of public health services, longer waiting time, and the lack of a convenient or nearby location of the facility. The poor are forced to seek private services which are more expensive and often foregone by the really poor. That is why cities that have better government hospitals and dispensaries and a better network of government medical auxiliary workers do better in terms of the availability of the service to the poorest quartile of the population. The eight-city study done in 2004–5 by the Ministry of Family Health and

Welfare provides some useful data that proves this to be the case. Table 26 shows the percentage of households in the eight cities using public health facilities for slum and non-slum areas as well as among the poorest quartile.

What is observable from Table 26 is that Chennai is the only city where the majority of households in the poorest quartile use government health facilities. In Mumbai, Hyderabad, and Kolkata around 40 per cent of such households do so. But for the remaining cities in this group, including Delhi, less than a third depend on government health facilities.

Turning to key indicators of healthcare availability among the three groups, Chennai does the best for maternal and infant care seen in the fact that the percentage of live births delivered in institutions is universal or 100 per cent among the poorest quartile, antenatal care visits are the norm for 99 per cent of such households, and the percentage of children between 0 to 71 months covered by *anganwadi* centres for such households is 97 per cent. Likewise, the percentage of children receiving vaccinations in slum areas is the highest of the eight cities at 89 per cent, higher than that in non-slum areas which was at 74 per cent.

TABLE 26 Percentage of Households Using Public Health Facilities in Slum and Non-slum Areas and in the Poorest Quartile, 2005–6

% of households	Chennai	Delhi	Hyderabad	Indore	Kolkata	Meerut	Mumbai	Nagpur
Slum	47	32	20	20	28	8	25	22
Non-slum	31	28	24	13	17	10	21	18
Poor	63	29	40	29	39	6	42	24

Source: Gupta et al. (2009).

No wonder then, Chennai's infant and child mortality was the least of all these eight cities at 28 and 35 deaths per thousand, respectively. However, Chennai still has to improve child nutrition as the percentage of underweight children and those with anaemia continue to be high among the poorest households in the city.

While persistent inequalities in access to basic health and disease prevention facilities remain a feature of the post-liberalized Indian city, a new challenge has emerged, competing for both resources and space in hospitals and clinics. These are the so-called 'lifestyle diseases', an offshoot of increasing incomes, sedentary lifestyles, and changes in diet. As the numbers of India's urban middle class keep rising, the numbers of those affected by such diseases also keep rising. One indicator is the proportion of those who are overweight or obese. The eight-city study provides some interesting data as shown in Table 27.

Break-up of the data by slum and non-slum areas was not given in the report although it was noted that the problem was greater in non-slum areas. In fact in non-slum areas, the percentage of women who are overweight or obese ranged from 23 per cent in Indore and Nagpur to 41 per cent in Chennai. Even in the

TABLE 27 Percentage of Women Aged 15–49 Who are Overweight or Obese, 2004–5

	Chennai	Delhi	Hyderabad	Indore	Kolkata	Meerut	Mumbai	Nagpur
% of overweight or obese women	39	27	33	22	30	30	27	19

Source: Gupta et al. (2009).

slum areas of Chennai and Hyderabad, around one-third of the women are overweight while in the other six cities between 14–25 per cent of the slum women are obese. While men as a whole have lower percentages of being overweight as compared to women, in Hyderabad and Chennai, one out of four men in non-slum areas is overweight. In the slum areas of these two cities, between 18–22 per cent of men are overweight.

What becomes clear from the above is that much more attention to diet and nutrition or the quality of food, for both the middle class as well as the poor, is needed as India's urban areas move out of the situation of absolute poverty where the quantity of food availability was of paramount importance. What is also seen is that southern cities such as Chennai and Hyderabad have higher levels of overweight population and this could partly be a reflection of local diets, ways of cooking and the choice of cooking medium.

Education

Although government and government-aided schools constitute the main type of school for primary and secondary levels of education in the country, in urban areas, private schools both aided and unaided play an important role. In fact, they have always played an important role with the best urban schools being private and generally run by missionaries. Data for the early 1990s indicate that in 1993–4 almost a third of primary schools (Classes 1–5) in urban areas were private, while at the upper primary level (Classes 6–8), it was nearly 50 per cent. At the secondary level, that is, Classes 8 till 10, nearly 68 per cent were private and at the higher secondary level, that is, Classes 10 to 12, almost 60 per cent were private. This pattern of private provision at higher levels of the schooling system is likely to have got stronger in the last fifteen years. In fact, the District Information System for Education (DISC) report for 2007 notes that this is the case.

Second, there tends to be much more diversity of education provision in cities as compared to rural areas. This is true for both the government-run schools and private schools. In urban areas, in addition to state-funded schools, there are municipal schools, state government schools, central schools (Kendriya Vidyalaya), and schools run for the children of various public sector employees such as those in the army, navy, air force, police, and railways. Some public sector companies such as BARC (Bhabha Atomic Research Centre), Atomic Energy Commission, Indian Airlines, and IOC (Indian Oil Corporation) run schools for the children of their staff. Regarding private schools, they are either affiliated to the state boards of education, the Central Board of Secondary Education (CBSC) or the Indian Certificate of School Education (ICSE). There are also schools run by embassies affiliated to overseas education boards and recently even some private schools have started offering both an Indian board/ foreign board option. To complicate matters, there may also be a number of unrecognized schools, particularly at the elementary level, feeding into secondary schools. There is also enrolment of children via correspondence courses in the national or state 'Open Schools'.

With this diverse range of schooling options, it is difficult to cover urban schooling adequately in a sub-section of a chapter and what is presented is of neces-sity brief and focused on a few aspects, for instance, the condition of urban elementary schools. The following analysis is largely based on the NUEPA's (National University of Educational Planning and Administration) data for elementary education in urban India in 2009–10. What we find is that, although progress has been made, there are still many deficiencies in physical infrastructure and school facilities as well as in indicators of enrolment and teacher quality. Starting with the most obvious, the condition of school buildings, at the national level about 77 per cent of urban elementary schools had a pucca building and another 5 per cent had a partially pucca building. Around 2 per cent of the schools still had no building. While the average number of classrooms has increased to around eight per school, around 3 per cent of the schools continue to operate in a single classroom and around 4 per cent are single-teacher schools. There has been a big improvement in the availability of drinking water in elementary schools, the national urban average being 96 per cent and it is mostly via tap (53 per cent) and hand pump (26 per cent). However, a gender bias in toilet facilities continues to persist with a functional girls' toilet in 77 per cent of the schools and a functional boys' toilet in 91 per cent of the schools. Only around 66 per cent of the elementary schools had playgrounds but where the elementary school was part of a larger school that had secondary and/or higher secondary levels, the presence of a playground was much more in evidence and 86 per cent of such schools did have one. Around 68 per cent of the schools had a book-bank or a small library, 46 per cent had a ground-level blackboard, and 43 per cent had a computer facility. Of course, there are significant variations among the states in all these figures. For instance, while in urban Kerala 90 per cent of elementary schools provide computers, in urban West Bengal it is a dismal 20 per cent. Regarding the percentage of schools having conducted a medical check-up last year, for urban Gujarat and Karnataka it is 90 per cent and 91 per cent, respectively, while for urban West Bengal and Bihar it is 28 and 20 per cent, respectively.

These data, however, would more accurately reflect conditions in state government schools and aided schools. As Juneja points out private schools and even some central government schools have not been very cooperative in the data-gathering exercises conducted by the NUEPA.

The overwhelming characteristic of schooling in urban India is the diversity of schools and their quality. Schools show great differences in their pedagogy, number of working days, attendance, teacher quality, and type of management. Likewise there is considerable diversity in learning achievement. The cost of schooling also shows wide variations, the least costly being government-run primary schools or municipal schools. Thus while there is increasing accessibility to primary education in India's cities, it is a 'differential accessibility' and not all types of schools are available to all. Those in the lowest socio-economic groups have limited choices. In fact, beyond the primary level, access to the poorest falls off sharply as there are fewer government-run schools at the upper primary and secondary levels. Thus their chances of continuing through the school system reduce drastically and completing the 10+2 years to gain a high school degree and then three more years for an undergraduate degree is still the stuff of dreams for the urban poor and the lower middle class.

The economic or class segregation that was noted in Chapter 4 in housing and other amenities has its origins in the differential chances of the children of better off and poorer families in accessing quality education and completing their studies. Creating separate schools for the poor and disadvantaged that are not up to the mark will continue to perpetuate this difference. To reduce the segregation by socioeconomic class that is so evident in urban schooling in India, all schools must be improved in terms of their quality and connectivity to secondary schools.

★ ★ ★

Indian cities have a long way to go before they become inclusive and offer a reasonably similar quality of life to all citizens. Tackling their ever-increasing populations has not made this task easy but with heightened economic growth and the availability of new and advanced technologies, the pursuit of a better quality of life for all should not be delayed any further. The state has an important role to play in aligning diverse and conflicting interests to promote strategies of urban growth and practices of urbanism that allow for equitable and sustainable development of its cities.

7

Future of Indian Cities

As India enters the second decade of the twenty-first century, it is faced with an inevitable urban transition. The magnitude of this transition and its many-layered impacts pose many challenges not only in terms of the matching of demand and supply of basic infrastructure and services, but also in terms of the kind of urban environment being created. There is need for greater effort to coordinate and integrate public as well as private actions to tackle the major problems cities are facing and to make them economically dynamic, inclusive, and sustainable. This will require assessing our current achievements and rethinking some key parameters. We will need to introspect much more about where urban development policy and planning is headed, and what kind of urbanism is being created and/or destroyed and its impact on the built environment as well as on the everyday life of urban residents.

Starting with a brief look at the way the present city came to be, Chapter 1 of this book provided a sweeping view of the development of urbanism in India from the earliest period in history to the recent past. Its purpose was to enable an understanding of what influences have shaped the characteristic way of life of city dwellers through time and in what ways they have changed. The self-regulatory, non-codified, and localized means of urban control that largely prevailed during pre-colonial times supported numerous types of small cities and towns, both inland and along the coast. City expansion was largely ad hoc and informal, as an organic response to local requirements and local climate. The colonial period, particularly after 1857, brought about a major shake-up in the pre-existing urban structure as new forms of settlement were introduced by the British along with the codification of rules and regulations for the formal administration of urban areas. Some networked urban infrastructure began to be laid in the civil lines and cantonment areas, which was later extended, in a piecemeal way, to sections of the native town. However, stark differences remained between the residence areas of the British and their administrative and military personnel and the locals. This dual pattern of urban development was inherited by the post-colonial state.

In the early decades after independence, there was a flurry to create more new towns to absorb the rising urban population and by the 1970s, around 112 new towns had been created. But they were still not sufficient and there was a growing shortage of land and housing in urban areas, relative to demand. Slums and squatter settlements grew to fill the gap and this process continues even after two decades of economic liberalization. A key focus of this book is the fact that city building processes in India have been a product of a planned response from the authorities as well as unplanned and ad hoc extensions made by both the poor and the middle classes to gain a foothold in the city. Any credible policy for the city must factor in both these processes.

Urban growth in the post-liberalization era, as discussed in Chapter 2, has started changing the look and feel of Indian cities. From glittering shopping malls, luxurious hotels, tall residential towers for the rich and upper middle class, the addition of numerous flyovers, and the ongoing construction of citywide metro systems, the top seven cities of the country have created new spaces to encompass the growing income and aspirations of an emerging 'middle class'. The growth of IT, ITES, and other new economy industries on the peripheries of the metropolitan area have increased job opportunities and enhanced the economic base of several cities. But, such growth has been uneven across the different urban regions of the country. While the western, southern, and the capital region around Delhi have done well in terms of the emergence of a dynamic new economy, much of the rest of the country and their urban areas have been bypassed. They have to get by on the old economy as well as a large informal sector. This is another incontrovertible fact and it is often lost sight of in the excitement of visualizing an emerging and 'shining India'. Chapter 3 focused on these activities highlighting the continued importance of the informal economy and its complementarities to the formal. Getting rid of the informal economy to give the cities a more global look would not make for sound economic policy as the growth of informal jobs exceeds that of formal jobs. Their coexistence would ensure continuity of a type of urbanism that is locality-based and responsive to the requirements of the diverse income classes that make up an Indian city.

Continuing with the formal–informal framework, Chapter 4 turned to the visual aspects of Indian cities and why they look the way they do. It identified two ongoing processes of change, gentrification and informalization, as occurring simultaneously to produce the hybrid cities that are typical of developing countries. In the case of India, the existence of many different cultures and religious practices within the urban population has produced an urban landscape of even greater diversity. Post 1980s, shifts in the economic structure of several leading cities from manufacturing to services have left their mark on the urban landscape as gigantic box-like shopping malls with their attendant residential towers and office space have taken over the vacant land left by closed factories and mills. They signal the increasing assertiveness of large developers and their standardized 'city models' which now loom higher in vertical height than the rest of the city and represent a new way of organizing space and of living the upper middle-class dream.

In Chapter 5 the focus was on urban dwellers. It has highlighted some important aspects of the social makeup of Indian cities and their influence in shaping the character of the city. A key to understanding the social make-up is to look at who lives where in the city and find out whether residential clustering has been on the basis of class, that is, income or on the basis of older groupings such as caste, religion, and mother tongue. Indian cities show considerable complexity in this regard for while there has been a broad shift to income-based choice of residence, which is not the case for Muslims, Scheduled Castes (SCs), and Scheduled Tribes (STs). Muslims continue to live in relative isolation in Muslim-dominant areas of the city which could either be in the old rundown core or in slums. In the case of SCs and STs, their higher poverty levels and lower levels of education have meant that they are predominantly found in the poorest areas such as slums and squatter settlements. This chapter also focused on migration, mainly from rural to urban areas and its role in changing the social composition of the city and as an avenue to better jobs and upward mobility.

In the final chapter, Chapter 6, we turned to the all-important issue of the quality of life in Indian cities and asked whether two decades of higher economic growth have translated into improved living conditions. Based on two recent all-India reports by the NSSO, the news is mixed. There has been steady improvement in the availability of water supply, sanitation, and electricity in urban areas. There has also been steady improvement in the quality of housing as seen in the switch from kutcha and semi-pucca to pucca. But pockets of uncovered population continue to exist and they are mostly in the slums and squatter settlements. In fact, other than water supply, there is a sharp drop in the availability of basic facilities and their quality within the lowest quintiles of per capita monthly consumption expenditure. The same pattern is repeated in the case of health services and education. To summarize this chapter, the quality of life of the middle and upper middle classes has been improving in the last two decades but in the case of the poor, Indian cities have a long way to go. Thus even two decades after heightened economic growth, much still remains to be done.

Now comes the inevitable question of not just what should be done but what should be done first. Among the myriad challenges facing Indian cities are several still uncompleted tasks carried over from the last century. These include several unfulfilled targets of providing universal access to decent basic services such as water supply, a clean and healthy environment, and a safe environment for work and living. Rather than on and off efforts at city 'beautification', these fundamental issues must remain a top priority for both city governments as well as the state. The health and safety of urban residents must precede all other concerns. That this is not so is seen in the enormous loss of life through negligence of basic issues such as fire safety that still continue to characterize urban living. The recent shocking death of ninety-one persons at a top-notch hospital in Kolkata due to lack of fire safety precautions amply testifies to the callous attitude of both the hospital owners and management as well as the state which had not enforced its own laws on fire safety. The state's role in ensuring public health and safety cannot be diluted in the name of privatization and markets.

Among other important actions to guide the future of Indian cities would be the selection of a strategy for their holistic growth keeping in mind their formal and informal components, the way these components complement each other and also compete with each other for space and economic mooring in the city.

They cater to the needs of different socioeconomic classes and together add to the capacity of the city to respond to diverse groups of people. They increase consumer choice and at the same time provide alternate experiences of the city. Together, they enhance the diversity of the city. Several global experts have repeatedly advised that informal ways of city expansion must be recognized and facilitated, as far as possible, rather than abruptly destroyed. A balance between formal and informal growth should be the basis of an urbanism of the future.

Third, focusing on the left-out poor pockets of the city and upgrading their basic services on an urgent basis is necessary for any sustained improvement of the city. The central government's JNNURM (Jawaharlal Nehru National Urban Renewal Mission) has a component designed to assist states financially do just this but state governments must follow through and sincerely implement the programme. Improvement in the quality of schools and health services in poor areas is also needed on an urgent basis.

It is also necessary to bring more social inclusiveness by improving the rundown Muslim enclaves that characterize most large Indian cities and increasing their educational and employment opportunities. Tying their improvement to the regeneration of historic districts could provide additional local income sources through improved tourism.

However, most importantly, there is need for a broad consensus on the choice of urban strategy for the city. This strategy should draw on the city's past and present to provide the basis for an urbanism that recognizes the local and incorporates it into city-building. It should keep in mind the fact that Indian cities have economically, socially, and culturally diverse populations. Our cities should continue to reflect this by providing a range of options to residents in the areas of housing, shopping, entertainment, health services, mode of travel, and so on.

Post liberalization there has been a big growth in large projects undertaken by large developers in the real estate market of India's metropolitan cities. Developer-driven large-scale city models have produced shopping, housing, and office space that has suited the needs of upper income households, the corporate sector, and an emerging class of new economy entrepreneurs. But will such standardized templates of city building be suitable for upgrading poorer areas in the city? Here a more nuanced and locality-based or a bottom–up approach should be used rather than the master-planned top–down approach that has been so successful in the case of corporate clients and the well-off. Imposing such a plan on poorer areas would simply lead to their being wiped out and a wholesale change in social composition.

Many Western countries today regret the loss of their earlier forms of urbanism, forms that were rooted in local needs and functions and some have even started reversing the spread of large-scale standardized city models. Thus the sterile landscape of excessive concrete use and parking lots is being replaced by more human-scale and people-friendly buildings in places such as suburban Toronto and Portland.

These are mistakes we can surely avoid as we make our urban transition. The best cities in the world are so because they are rooted in a locally based urbanism and built through incremental learning and adjustment. They are environmentally balanced and responsive to the needs of the local climate. In the haste to fill costly urban land with iconic towers, Indian cities should not lose their 'horizontality' or their links to the ground and its social and climatic exigencies. Keeping a sense of horizontality will make for more comfortable living spaces for, as pointed out by Dalvi, no amount of steel and glass can compensate for natural shade, sunshine, and cross-ventilation in the tropics.

Indian cities would do well to make liveability their ultimate goal rather than the chimera of global city tags as we still have a long way to go before many basic problems are solved and our cities are satisfactory living habitats for all urban dwellers.

References

Introduction

Hosagrahar, Jyoti. 2005. *Indigenous Modernities: Negotiating Architecture and Urbanism*. London: Routledge.

Mehrotra, Rahul. 2008. 'Negotiating the Static and Kinetic Cities: The Emergent Urbanism of Mumbai', in Andreas Huyssen (ed.), *Other Cities, Other Worlds: Urban Imaginaries in a Globalizing Age*, pp. 205–18. Durham: Duke University Press.

Chapter 1

For Ancient India

Kosambi, D.D. 1965. *Ancient India: A History of Its Culture and Civilization*. New York: Pantheon Books; Singh, Yogendra. 1977. *Modernization of Indian Tradition*. Faridabad:

Thomson Press; Smith, Monica L. 2006. 'The Archaeology of South Asian Cities', *Journal of Archaeological Research*, 14: 97–142; Thapar, Romila. 1987. *A History of India*. Vol. 1. London: Penguin Books.

For Medieval India

Hambly, Gavin, R.G. 1984. 'Towns and Cities: Mughal India', in Tapan Raychaudhuri and Irfan Habib (eds), *The Cambridge Economic History of India, Vol. 1, c. 1200–c. 1750*, pp. 434–51. Hyderabad: Orient Longman; Parasher, Aloka. 1991. 'Social Structure and Economy of Settlements in the Central Deccan (200 B.C.–A.D. 200)', in Indu Banga (ed.), *The City in Indian History: Urban Demography, Society, and Politics*, pp. 19–46. New Delhi: Manohar Publications.

For Colonial India

Hosagrahar, Jyoti. 2005. *Indigenous Modernities: Negotiating Architecture and Urbanism*. London: Routledge.

For Post-colonial India till 1991

Ramachandran, R. 1989. *Urbanization and Urban Systems in India*. New Delhi: Oxford University Press; Shaw, Annapurna. 1996. 'Urban Policy in Post-independent

India: An Appraisal', *Economic and Political Weekly,* 31(4): 224–8; Shaw, Annapurna. 2009. 'Town Planning in India, 1947–1965: Chandigarh Reexamined', *Urban Geography,* 30(8): 857–78; Sita, K. and R.B. Bhagat. 2007. 'Population Change and Economic Restructuring in Indian Metropolitan Cities: A Study of Mumbai', in Annapurna Shaw (ed.), *Indian Cities in Transition.* Hyderabad: Orient Longman; Sivaramakrishnan, K.C., Amitabh Kundu, and B.N. Singh. 2005. *Handbook of Urbanization in India.* New Delhi: Oxford University Press.

Chapter 2

Shaw, Annapurna. 1999. 'Emerging Patterns of Urban Growth in India', *Economic and Political Weekly,* 34 (16 & 17): 969–78.

———. 2005. 'Peri-urban Interface of Indian Cities: Growth, Governance and Local Initiatives', *Economic and Political Weekly,* 40(2): 129–36.

———. 2007. 'Metropolitan Restructuring in Post-liberalized India: Separating the Global and the Local', *Cities: The Journal of Urban Policy and Planning,* 24(2): 148–63.

Yardley, Jim. 2011. 'In India, Dynamism Wrestles with Dysfunction', *New York Times,* 9 June 2011. Available at http://www.nytimes.com/2011/06/09/world/asia/09gurgaon.html?pagewanted=all.

Chapter 3

Himangshu. 2007. 'Urban Poverty in India by Size-class of Towns: Level, Trends and Characteristics'. Available at www.csh-delhi.com/team/downloads/publ, accessed on 5 April 2011.

Mukhopadhyay, Partha. 2011. 'Formality and Functionality in Indian Cities'. Available at http://www.india-seminar.com/2011/617/617_partha_mukhopadhyay.htm, accessed on 4 August 2011.

Chapter 4

Brosius, Christiane. 2010. *India's Middle Class: New Forms of Urban Leisure, Consumption and Prosperity*. Routledge: New Delhi.

Brugmann, Jeb. 2009. *Welcome to the Urban Revolution: How Cities are Changing the World*. Noida: HarperCollins Publishers India.

Lang, Jon, Madhavi Desai, and Miki Desai. 1997. *Architecture and Independence: The Search for Identity, India 1880–1980*. New Delhi: Oxford University Press.

Mehrotra, Rahul. 2008. 'Negotiating the Static and Kinetic Cities: The Emergent Urbanism of Mumbai', in Andreas Huyssen (ed.), *Other Cities, Other Worlds: Urban Imaginaries in a Globalizing Age*, pp. 205–18. Durham: Duke University Press.

Nair, Janaki, 2007. *Bangalore's Twentieth Century: The Promise of the Metropolis*. New Delhi: Oxford University Press.

Neuwirth, Robert. 2005. *Shadow Cities: A Billion Squatters, A New Urban World*. New York: Routledge.

Roy, Ananya. 2008. *Calcutta Requiem: Gender and the Politics of Poverty*. New Delhi: Pearson Longman.

Sivam, Alpana and Karuppannan Sadasivam. 2002. 'Role of State and Market in Housing Delivery for Low-income Groups in India', *Journal of Housing and the Built Environment,* 17: 69–88.

Urban Age. 2007. *Housing Typologies in Mumbai*. Available at http://www.urban-age.net/10_cities/07_mumbai/mumbai_HT.html.

Chapter 5

Bhagat, R.B. and Soumya Mohanty. 2009. 'Emerging Pattern of Urbanization and the Contribution of Migration in Urban Growth in India', *Asian Population Studies,* 5(1): 5–18.

Bose, N.K. 1968. *Calcutta 1964: A Social Survey*. Bombay: Lalvani Publishing.

Chauduri, Sukanta (ed.) 1990. *Calcutta: The Living City*, Vol. 2. New Delhi: Oxford University Press.

De Neve and Henrike Donner (eds) 2006. *The Meaning of the Local: Politics of Place in Urban India*. London: Routledge.

Dupont, Veronique. 2004. 'Socio-spatial Differentiation and Residential Segregation in Delhi: A Question of Scale?', *Geoforum*, 35: 157–75.

Dyson, Tim and Pravin Visaria. 2004. 'Migration and Urbanization: Retrospect and Prospects', in Tim Dyson, Robert Cassen, and Leela Visaria (eds), *Twenty-first Century India: Population, Economy, Human Development and the Environment*, pp. 108–29. New Delhi: Oxford University Press.

Gupta, Kamla, Fred Arnold, and H. Lhungdim. 2009. 'Health and Living Conditions in Eight Indian Cities', *National Family Health Survey (NFHS-3)-2005–6*. Mumbai: International Institute of Population Sciences.

Gyan, Prakash. 2010. *Mumbai Fables.* New Delhi: HarperCollins Publishers India.

Himangshu. 2006. 'Urban Poverty in India by Size-class of Towns: Levels, Trends and Characteristics', Centre de Sciences Humaines, Delhi. Available at http://www.csh-delhi.com/team/downloads/publiperso/urban_IGIDR_paper.pdf.

Kosambi, Meera. 1986. *Bombay in Transition: The Growth and Social Ecology of a Colonial City, 1880–1980.* Stockholm: Almqvist & Wiksell International.

Mahadevia, Darshini. 2007. 'A City with Many Borders: Beyond Ghettoisation in Ahmedabad', in Annapurna Shaw (ed.), *Indian Cities in Transition,* pp. 341–89. Hyderabad: Orient Longman.

Mathur, Om Prakash. 2009. *National Urban Poverty Reduction Strategy 2010–2020 A.D.: Slum-free Cities.* New Delhi: The National Institute of Public Finance and Policy. Available at http://www.nipfp.org.in/opm_files/ opmathur/Final%20Poverty%20Rep.pdf.

Naidu, Ratna. 1990. *Old Cities, New Predicaments: A Study of Hyderabad.* New Delhi: Sage Publications.

Neetha, N. 2011. 'Closely Woven: Domestic Work and Internal Migration of Women in India', in S. Irudaya Rajan (ed.), *Migration, Identity and Conflict: India Migration Report 2011,* pp. 219–35. New Delhi: Routledge.

Seabrook, Jeremy and Imran Ahmed Siddiqui. 2011. *People without History: India's Muslim Ghettos.* New Delhi: Navayana Publishing.

Singh, D.P. 2009. 'Poverty and Migration: Does Moving Help?', in Ministry of Housing and Urban Poverty Alleviation and UNDP, *India Urban Poverty Report 2009,* pp. 50–75. New Delhi: Oxford University Press.

Vithayathil, Trina and Gayatri Singh. 2011. 'Spaces of Discrimination: Residential Segregation in Indian Cities', paper for the Population Association of America meeting, Washington, DC. Available at http://paa2011.princeton. edu/download.aspx?submissionId=112174.

Chapter 6

Government of India, National Sample Survey Office (NSSO). 2010. 'Housing Condition and Amenities in India 2008–9', Report No. 535 (65th Round).

———. 2010. 'Some Characteristics of Urban Slums, 2008–9', Report No. 534 (65th Round).

Gupta, Kamla, Fred Arnold, and H.Lhungdim. 2009. 'Health and Living Conditions in Eight Indian Cities', *National Family Health Survey (NFHS-3)—2005–6*. Mumbai: International Institute of Population Sciences.

Juneja, Nalini. 2011. 'Access to What? Diversity and Participation', in R. Govinda (ed.), *Who Goes to School? Exploring Exclusion in Indian Education*, pp. 205–47. New Delhi: Oxford University Press.

Chapter 7

Brugmann, Jeb. 2009. *Welcome to the Urban Revolution: How Cities are Changing the World*. Noida: HarperCollins Publishers India.

Dalvi, Mustansir. 2011. 'The Blue Tarpaulin—What It Bares about Mumbai's Highrises'. Available at http://www.firstpost.com/mumbai/the-blue-tarpaulin-what-it-bares-about-mumbais-high-rises-153671.html.

Neuwirth, Robert. 2005. *Shadow Cities: A Billion Squatters, A New Urban World*. New York: Routledge.

Satterthwaite, David. 2010. 'Upgrading Slums: With and for Slum-dwellers', *Economic and Political Weekly*, 45(10): 12–16.

Index